# A Winter's Tale

### THE WRECK OF
### THE *FLORIZEL*

# A Winter's Tale

## THE WRECK OF THE *FLORIZEL*

## Cassie Brown

DOUBLEDAY CANADA LIMITED
Toronto, Ontario
DOUBLEDAY & COMPANY, INC.
Garden City, New York

1976

ISBN: 0-385-12570-4
Library of Congress Catalog Card Number: 76-20386

FIRST EDITION

Book design by Robert Garbutt Productions
Printed in Canada by The Alger Press Limited

*Photographs courtesy of:*

The Collier family, the Taylor family, the Timmons
family, Mrs. John Johnston, Mrs. Philip Jackman,
Mrs. Tommy Williams, Mrs. J. Goobie, Mrs. F. Davis,
Mr. Ted Drover, Mr. Burnham Gill, Mr. Ron Young,
Captain Tom Goodyear, Mr. Varrick Frissell Cox,
Tooton's Limited, Mr. Frank Kennedy, Mr. Martin
Lee, Miss M. W. Stone, William B., and Robert J.
Martin, Mrs. George Brown, Mrs. Vincent Maloney,
Mrs. Dermott Crockwell, Department of Energy,
Mines and Resources, and from the author's private
collection.
 The course of the *S.S. Florizel* was mapped by
Captain Tom Goodyear.

*To those passengers and crew of the* S.S. Florizel *who showed indomitable courage in the face of disaster, this book is dedicated.*

AUTHOR'S NOTE

THIS IS A true story. Evidence of 55 wit-
nesses has been taken from the Marine Court of Enquiry held in March and April, 1918, and in private
interviews with five of the survivors.

Information was also collected from the files of the
*Daily News*, the *Evening Telegram*, the *Evening Advocate*,
and the *Daily Star* of St. John's; the Newfoundland Arc-
hives, and the Department of Justice. Other sources in-
clude the Meteorological Branch of the Department of
Transport; Richard Nelis, Meteorologist; C. F. Rowe,
Meteorologist.

The following people provided details in interviews
taped in 1972, 1973, and 1975: Captain Tom Goodyear,
Ron Young, Alex Ledingham, Mrs. Michael McDonald,
(nee Kitty Cantwell); Mrs. Philip Jackman, Captain
Eugene Burden, Jim Myrick, R. A. (Dick) Harvey, the
Herbert Taylor family, St. John's; and Dave Griffiths,
Long Harbour, Placentia Bay; John Metcalfe, Topsail,
Conception Bay; Samuel Cooper, Fort Lauderdale,
Florida. The story of Mrs. Henry Kraph, (nee Minnie
Denief), Brooklyn, N.Y., was compiled through letters
to the author in 1963. Burnham Gill, Len Murphy, John
Doyle, the George Crocker family, the Billy Guzzwell

family, St. John's; the Gregory Maloney family, the James Crockwell family, Bay Bulls, also provided color stories.

For vital assistance in other ways, the author thanks William and Daphne Rolls, Traytown, Bonavista Bay; Alma King, St. John's; and Laurie and Billie Brown, Clarenville, Trinity Bay.

C.B.
St. John's, Newfoundland.

# CONTENTS

*ix*

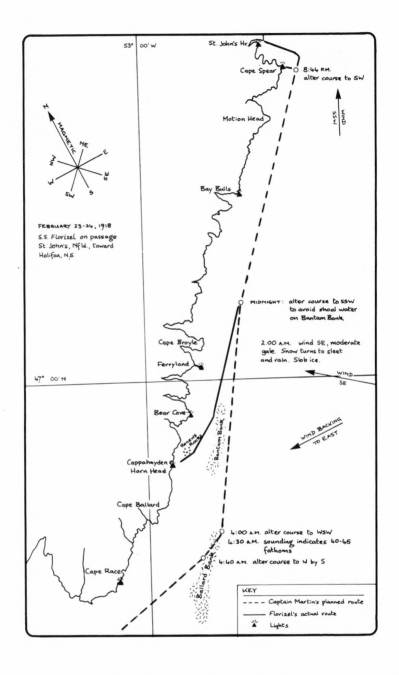

53° 00' W

St. John's Hr.

Cape Spear — 8:44 P.M.
alter course to SW

SSW WIND

Motion Head

N MAGNETIC NE NNW E ESE W SW S

FEBRUARY 23-24, 1918
S.S. Florizel on passage
St. John's, Nfld., toward
Halifax, N.S.

Bay Bulls

MIDNIGHT: alter course to SSW
to avoid shoal water
on Bantam Bank

2.00 A.M. wind SE, moderate
gale. Snow turns to sleet
and rain. Slob ice.

Cape Broyle

Ferryland

47° 00' N

WIND SE

Bear Cove

WIND BACKING TO EAST

Renews Rock

Bantam Bank

Cappahayden &
Horn Head

Cape Ballard

4:00 A.M. alter course to WSW

4:30 A.M. sounding indicates 40-45
fathoms

4:40 A.M. alter course to W by S

Ballard Bank

Cape Race

KEY
- - - - Captain Martin's planned route
——— Florizel's actual route
⚓ Lights

ONWARD SHE CAME, pitching and rolling wildly through the sleet-ridden blackness of night. Great seas rose up around her, hurled their smoking crests upon her deck in drenching sheets of icy spray. She heeled viciously to port and back to starboard so that all was chaos in her belly.

But she was a sturdy ship. She had shown her mettle during worse storms in the North Atlantic, and she shook off the heavy seas, smacked them resoundingly, her flat-bottomed bow riding easily over them.

On the bridge an order was given, the course altered, and her bow swung landward. Bounding through the furious seas, the *S. S. Florizel* struck Horn Head Point off Cappahayden on the southeast coast of Newfoundland. Impaled on the rocks with her back broken, the bottom torn out of her, the ship began to disintegrate while her 78 passengers and 60 crew members fought for their lives. Ninety-four died.

*Exactly what happened on the* Florizel *throughout the night of February 23-24, 1918, was to remain a mystery for more than half a century.* This book tells the story of that fateful night.

PART I

# The Discards
# and
# The Chosen

# CHAPTER 1

*FATE, THE* weaver, selected with infinite patience and delicacy a thread here, a thread there, uniting the various strands of life into a pattern of disaster. One hundred and thirty-eight souls would be tried and tested by the terrible destiny that awaited them. Others would be discarded before the design was complete — only later would they know that Fate spared them.

The time was February, 1918. World War I was in its fourth year but Armistice was still nine months away. Urgent pleadings from Great Britain were producing a steady trickle of young men from the bays and coves around Newfoundland, despite the fact that most of her own volunteer regiment had been slaughtered like sacrificial lambs at infamous Beaumont Hamel, July 1, 1916. Some of these volunteers would be chosen to play a role in this disaster.

The rendezvous was Newfoundland, that craggy sentinel of the western world. Geographically, the island lay at the tail end of the Caribbean storm path. Moist tropical winds flowing northward grew rough and troublesome when they collided with the dry, cold air of the north, increasing in strength and boisterousness so that by the time they reached Newfoundland they had developed into full-blown storms with furious winds, rain, sleet, and snow. This winter there had been little reprieve from storms that wracked the island. In addition, the Polar Current nudged rocky shores with the ice pack and beleaguered the island for long, harsh weeks. Shifting winds, tides, and currents frequently caused the ice pack to squeeze and crush ships like matchwood; shipping lanes around the coast had to be navigated with extreme caution.

The victim chosen for this experience was the S. S. *Florizel*, of the prestigious Bowring's Red Cross Line, a large, sturdy ship of 3,081 tons gross weight, 305 feet in length with a 42-foot beam. She had four decks, four holds, and accommodations for 145 first-class and 36 second-class passengers. She was splendidly furnished, richly carpeted, upholstered in plush, finished in oak and mahogany and costly green tapestry. Sea voyages on Bowring's Red Cross Line were popular with the traveling public. The food was outstanding, and the crew members appeared to be a close-knit family unit, radiating warmth, friendliness, and concern for the creature comforts of the passengers. A special feature was her automatic whistle, which could give eight long blasts a minute, and it was of great service when the steamer was making Long Island Sound or the Newfoundland coast — both equally *in*famous for their fog.

Built primarily as a passenger liner, she was designed, it was said, like a codfish to cope with ice because she was used as a sealing ship in the spring of each year. She was also one of the world's first fleet of icebreakers. She had a triple-expansion engine with cylinders of 24 inches, 40 inches, and 64 inches diameter, and a 42-inch stroke and 180 pounds pressure fed by three boilers. Her bunker capacity was 450 tons — small by today's standards, but in 1909 she was the pride of Bowring's fleet.

The yearly trips to the icefields for the slaughter of seals were by far her most lucrative ventures. Her trip to the ice in 1910 netted her a record-breaking 49,000 seal pelts. During the seal hunt rough boards protected the decks from the sealers' hobnailed boots, and her elegant saloons and staterooms were locked against invasion by the seal hunters. who lived in her cargo holds.

Because of the war she had not gone to the seal hunt since 1915, but she had crossed the Atlantic several times with volunteers for the slaughter that was taking place in Europe. The *Florizel's* main function, however, was the St. John's - Halifax - New York run, with the odd Caribbean cruise thrown in. The agents who booked passengers and cargo were Harvey and Company, Ltd., a large and prestigious firm.

The S. S. *Florizel* was overdue on her return trip from New York and Halifax. Stormy seas had forced her to run at reduced speed throughout most of the voyage, putting her a day behind schedule.

In spite of the rough weather, this particular trip was an exciting one. Among the passengers was the shipwrecked crew of the vessel *Lottie Silver*, whose seamen had gripping tales to tell of many near-scrapes with death aboard a derelict vessel battered by savage seas.

Listening to these stories were two young New York doctors named Knowlton and Bartecou. They were going to the icefields in March; Knowlton would make the trip with Captain William Winsor in the *Thetis*, Bartecou would go in the *Neptune* with Captain George Barbour. It was Bartecou's first trip to Newfoundland and the icefields, but Knowlton had been going for three or four years, lured northward, undoubtedly, by the spectacular 1914 tragedy of seal hunters who had frozen to death on the icefield. If they hoped to be spectators to another grim adventure, one of them would have his wish fulfilled.

Another source of excitement, coupled with fear, had come with the outbreak of smallpox on board ship. Twenty-four hours from port it was discovered that the chef had contracted the disease, and eight other crew members* were suspected of having it. The *Florizel* was also minus a chief steward this trip. Steward Francis H. Jones had been taken ill and sent to hospital in New York to undergo surgery.

On Tuesday, February 19, the *Florizel* steamed in through The Narrows and into the harbor of St. John's, dropping anchor at midstream in the quarantine grounds to await the arrival of the port physicians, who came presently with enough vaccine to inoculate the whole ship. Only on the following day was she permitted to haul alongside the wharf and discharge those passengers and crew members who carried vaccination certificates. The chef went to hospital; the other crew members were taken ashore and put into isolation along with a handful of passengers.

The *Florizel* was fumigated at the cost of 5,000 dollars.

Smallpox was still the dreaded scourge it had been for centuries, but health authorities were now acknowledging the wisdom of vaccination. In most major ports of call in North America, certificates were demanded before travelers from foreign lands could set foot ashore. The island of Newfoundland, being a colony of Great Britain, was considered a foreign land by continental America, and Newfoundlanders traveling to the continent required inoculations.

Although smallpox vaccination was first introduced

---

* Chief Officer John Edward Tucker, Stewardess Ethel McHardy, Richard Best, James Viscount, Alex Janes, Harry Freeman, A. Walsh and H. Chaytor, cooks and stewards.

in Trinity Bay, Newfoundland, as far back as 1800, it was still not mandatory for Newfoundlanders to have it; therefore few willingly underwent the discomfort of it unless absolutely forced to do so. Canada and the United States required vaccinations, and, since fumigation was a costly affair, so did the Red Cross Line. Consequently, when travelers presented themselves at the ticket office at Harvey's for the next sailing of the *Florizel*, they were informed that, before they could set foot aboard, they were required to have the vaccination.

Thus did Fate intervene.

Many promptly canceled their sea voyage. Businessman W. B. Grieve, plagued by ill health, was advised by his physician not to risk inoculation. Mr. and Mrs. Harry E. Cowan, Mr. and Mrs. Peter Cowan, T. J. Duley, H. R. Brookes, Mrs. F. J. Fanning and her two children, Mrs. C. McKay Harvey, J. Dewling, George Kearney, F. Steer, and John J. Duff, all prominent in the business and social world of St. John's, refused to comply with the new regulation.

Inspector-General and Mrs. Charles Henry Hutchings had been planning a trip to the United States, fully intending to take passage on the *Florizel*, but for no particular reason decided to wait until her next trip. A contingent of 60 volunteers, in training at army camp on the outskirts of St. John's, were scheduled to sail to Halifax, where they would embark via another transport for the war overseas. They would be scratched from the list in the last hours before sailing.

The process of discarding had begun.


Another storm battered the island on Wednesday. Strong southwest winds blew off rooftops, shattered windows, and brought sleet, snow, and sub-zero temperatures. Friday, February 22, was a brisk day with fresh west winds and warming temperatures, but southward, warm moist winds flowing up from the Gulf of Mexico collided with a cold, dry front pressing down over the United States from Canda. This created wind, rain, sleet, and a roll of low dark cloud over the Great Lakes and down to the southern States.

High above the cold front, the warm air began a cyclonic anti-clockwise motion, forming a great rotating funnel-shaped cloud mass that rose and spread above the continent. Spinning and deepening, it moved eastward to Cape Hatteras on the North Carolina coast.

It was duly noted by the Meteorological Office in Toronto, Canada, and warnings were issued to the eastern seaboard.

# CHAPTER 2

*THE CLERK* at the Red Cross Line office was quite explicit: no vaccination certificate, no ticket. Edgar Froude regretfully canceled his trip on the *Florizel*. He did not like the idea of coping with the complications that beset newly vaccinated people, not on a business trip during which he would need all of his faculties.

"Then I will go by *train*," he said firmly, and immediately went to the railway station to arrange the trip across the island — a tiresome, jolting journey of 600 miles on a narrow-gauge railway followed by a 12-hour voyage across the Cabot Strait to North Sydney in a cramped, stuffy little steamer. It was not the most pleasant prospect.

"It is quite possible, sir," the railway clerk informed him, "that port officials in North Sydney will also require your being vaccinated."

Edgar Froude bowed to Fate. "If I must be vaccinated then I must, so I will have the pleasure of a sea voyage and sail on the *Florizel*."

In reverse, James H. Baggs, a wealthy merchant in the booming herring industry, had already made the rough journey from Newfoundland's west coast to St.

John's in order to sail on the *Florizel*. It would have been much quicker if he had taken the train westward, a mere 142 miles from his home town, crossed the Cabot Strait on the gulf steamer to North Sydney, and entrained there for New York. In fact, that had been his original plan, but snowstorms on the Gaff Topsails (the highest point of land over which the railway ran) had blocked all train movements for days. The first train that got through had come from the west coast heading for St. John's, and Baggs had changed his plans on the spot, deciding to go on to St. John's and take a ship from there. As the newspapers were later to word it, "Fate plays some strange tricks and none stranger than in the case of James H. Baggs."

Fred Snow, a corporal in the Canadian Army, had transferred to the Imperial Flying Corps. His cousin, Edward Berteau — son of the Auditor-General, F. C. Berteau — and good friends Frank Chown, Jack Parsons, and Newman Sellars had indicated that they, too, were joining the Flying Corps to fight for King and Country, but they had continually postponed breaking the ties with home. Fred decided to go anyway and was scheduled to leave St. John's by train with an uncle who was going to Canada on business. His friends decided that they had delayed long enough and, as a group, booked passage to Halifax on the *Florizel*. They urged young Snow to forego the railway journey and sail with them, and a few hours before departure, he decided to do so.

George Parmiter was sailing to Halifax to join the Canadian Army. Lieutenant Ralph Burnham, a seasoned soldier who had already served with the fighting forces overseas, had fractured a leg during maneuvers. On recovery he had transferred to the Royal Flying Corps, and had been granted a short leave with his parents in St. John's before going on to Canada for special training. His leave was now over and he, too, was on his way to Halifax.

Gerald St. John, a first-year student at St. Mary's in Halifax, hated college and on his arrival home at Christmas had been determined not to return. His parents had been equally determined that he would. On the previous trip of the *Florizel*, he had jumped ship at the last moment. This time his parents planned to remain aboard ship with him until the last possible moment, disembarking just before the gangplank was removed. This time, Gerald would sail.

Major Michael S. Sullivan, a civil engineer, distinguished in business and politics, had been commissioned in 1916 to form and take charge of a Newfoundland Forestry Corps with headquarters near Dunkeld, Perthshire, Scotland. He had done so with excellent results, and in January had returned to Newfoundland to recruit more volunteers for the Forestry Division. Now recalled to London, he was booked on the *Florizel* for Halifax to return for duty in the British Isles. His wife and two children, living in Montreal, had been granted special permission to join him in Halifax and sail to England with him.

George Massie, a Scotsman in the fish business, now a resident of Chicago, had visited Newfoundland's west coast to study the herring fishery. On this trip he had brought his wife and daughter. His business concluded, Massie and his family planned to sail home on the *Florizel*.

Captain O. P. Belleveau of Weymouth, Nova Scotia, had sailed Bowring's new three-masted schooner, *Gwendolyn Warren*, to St. John's. He worked frantically to finish his business with Bowring's so that he could sail on the *Florizel*. He succeeded. Noah Dauphinee, of Tantillion County, Nova Scotia, mate of the *Gwendolyn*

*Warren*, would return on the same voyage.

Captain James Bartlett, John Forest, Charles Howell, and James Stockley were sailing to Halifax to bring a vessel, the *Jessie Ashley*, to St. John''s for a business firm. Captain Bartlett, aged 25, had survived shipwreck a couple of times.

Gregory Maloney, James Crockwell, George Puddester, and John Lynch of Bay Bulls were sailing to Halifax to engage in construction work. Halifax had been flattened by the explosion of the munitions ship *Mont Blanc*, when it collided with the Norwegian relief ship, *Imo*, in December, 1917, and the city was desperately in need of good carpenters. The four men had decided to work together.

Maloney and Crockwell, first cousins, had grown up together, worked together, and were as prosperous as the times permitted. Maloney, Puddester, and Lynch were married; Crockwell, 41, was not, although he was to be married within the year.

Maloney, a handsome man of middle years, did not enjoy the prospect of having to leave his family, but winter work was scarce and he had seven children to feed. His wife Mary, six months pregnant, sensibly agreed that it was the practical thing to do. She was a contented woman, her husband was solidly dependable, a good provider, and held in great esteem in the little outport. "You go," she told him when he had first broached the subject.

"Take good care of your mother," he told 14-year-old Albert as he was leaving for the train.

"I will, sir."

Mary said, "We'll be all right, Greg."

Dave Griffiths of Long Harbour, Placentia Bay, home from the United States for the past 14 months because of illness, suddenly made the decision to return to the

States. At dawn on Saturday, February 23, he left home, carrying a suitcase, and walked 14 miles to Placentia Junction to catch the train to St. John's, 90 miles away.

The same train picked up two Navy men at the next station. Home on furlough from the Dardanelles since early January, Samuel Cooper and Walter Reid had been stranded in Trinity Bay because of the storms. Cooper had wisely cabled for a 10-day extension of leave from Commander Anthony MacDermott of the *Briton*, Naval Reserve Headquarters in St. John's. Walter Reid had not, so to all intents and purposes he was AWOL and in trouble. It didn't bother Reid: it had not been physically possible for him to get back to St. John's, so what could the Navy do about it?

The Master-at-Arms told Cooper and Reid what he thought of them in no uncertain terms, and promised he would get them back into the war quicker than they had bargained for. "Be ready to sail on the *Florizel* tonight," he barked.

The two sailors were not intimidated; Cooper was actually looking forward to getting back into action. He had spent two years in the Dardanelles; two ships had been torpedoed and sunk beneath him, he had gone from one action to another and had lost all sense of fear; action had become a way of life with him. It was the same with Walter Reid. Next time they might not be so lucky, but until then they weren't worrying about it.

Peter Guilfoyle, a seaman who sailed out of New York as a member of the American Merchant Navy, had been home on compassionate leave because his father was dying. Now it was all over and Peter made the decision to return to the States on this trip of the *Florizel*.

Stewardess Margaret Keough* of the S. S. *Prospero*

* Also spelled Kehoe.

was called upon to fill the place of Ethel McHardy, hospitalized with smallpox. Captain William James, Master of the S. S. *Ranger*, a ship being readied for the impending seal hunt, was called upon to replace Chief Officer John Tucker, also ill. Second Steward Charles Snow would take over the duties of Chief Steward Jones (recuperating in hospital in New York), and Waiter Henry Snow, Charles' brother, would become acting second steward. Charles had also commandeered his brother-in-law, Fred Roberts, to fill a vacancy left by the third cook, who was under quarantine. Michael Dunphy, formerly a steerage steward on the S. S. *Portia*, also replaced one of the *Florizel* stewards in quarantine, since the *Portia* had been taken for foreign service some weeks back.

Saturday the 23rd was cold. Although the early-morning thermometer registered only 13 degrees above zero, a ridge of high pressure, extending from the South Atlantic, brought eastern Newfoundland pleasant weather. But the warnings from Toronto had been received and storm signals were aloft on wind-scoured Signal Hill, warning all that another blow was on the way.

Southward, the storm was now off Cape Hatteras, intensifying and contracting upon itself until it was a whirlpool of condensing moisture that fell in a deluge around the center. The storm began to spin up along the eastern seaboard toward Newfoundland, the fringes cooling as it sucked in the cold winds of the north, chilling the warm air and converting its moisture to sleet and snow. By 9:00 A.M. on Saturday the front had reached Sable Island, which was reporting southeasterly gales of 45 knots.

It was not a severe storm, merely one of the family of storms that had plagued the island for weeks — but its offspring, a heavy ocean swell, was giving spectacular evidence of its existence as it smashed against the south coast of Newfoundland.

It did not worry the owners of the *Florizel* that their number-one ship was due to head out into the storm. It certainly did not appear to worry those passengers who were scheduled to sail on her. The *Florizel* had proved her worth many times over; she handled herself well in all kinds of weather.

Scheduled departure was 4:00 P.M.

There were some last-minute changes in the passenger list. Samuel Cooper and Walter Reid on the *Briton* were brusquely informed that their sailing orders had been canceled. The 60 volunteers headed for Halifax and overseas were scratched, but William Earle, Michael O'Driscoll, William Moore, and George A. (Bert) Moulton made a last-minute appearance. Moulton, father of seven-year-old Clarence B. Moulton, a deaf mute attending school in Halifax, had brought young Clarence aboard earlier, expecting to put him, as he usually did, in the charge of Stewardess Ethel McHardy. Clarence had taken one look at the unfamiliar stewardess and kicked up such a ruckus that George Moulton had hurried home, hastily packed a bag, and bought a ticket for Halifax.

Wilbert Butler, shipwright and diver, commissioned by a St. John's firm to work on the refloating of one of their ships which had grounded on the Florida Keys, had been unable to secure a ticket for passage until the cancellations had rolled in.

For this trip the *Florizel* had 78 passengers, nine of them women and six children. Of the children, Blanche Beaumont, 11 years old and blind, and Clarence Moulton, were headed for the Halifax schools for the Blind, and the Deaf and Dumb. Eleven-year-old William

Guzzwell was joining his mother in New York. Widowed early in life, she had moved to New York, had recently remarried, and had sent for Billy. Katherine Massie, aged eight, was returning to Chicago with her parents; for her return to the mainland, Katherine had to be vaccinated before she sailed. Betty Munn, not yet four years old, was in the charge of her nurse, Evelyn Trenchard. Betty's mother had gone to New York in early January for surgery, and Betty and her father, John Shannon Munn, were joining her. They planned to continue on to Florida, where Mrs. Munn would recuperate in the sunshine. Baby John Maloney was the seven-month-old son of Joseph and Mary Maloney.

Of the nine female passengers, Annie Dalton was on her way to New York and a new job. Kitty Cantwell, a good friend of Annie's was on a pleasure trip to the great city to visit her sister. Mabel Barrett, a beautiful, statuesque young woman, was going away to live with her sister in New York; an early marriage had ended disastrously and she was getting away from it all. Minnie Denief was going to New York to live with her sister and to find work. Elizabeth Pelley of Smith Sound, Trinity Bay, was also going to live and work in New York.

The most prominent passenger was John Shannon Munn, Managing Director of the Red Cross Line, and of Bowring Brothers. At the age of 37, he wielded the power and received the veneration usually reserved for older men. Not only was he a scholar, but it was said his ideas had gone into the design of the *Florizel*.

The daily newspapers warned of the approaching storm: "Winds increasing to gales from east and northeast with snow, clearing again early on Sunday."

With the storm signals flying there was some question among the crew as to whether or not the *Florizel* might lie over until it had passed. Shortly after midday, the 4:00 P.M. departure was delayed until seven-thirty that evening.

Captain William Martin, 43, was a careful navigator. In fact, the crew often told him he was *too* careful. He was reputed never to leave the bridge in stormy weather, and since the war he'd seldom left it in fine weather. It had been said, among his friends, that he never felt at ease when eating with the passengers but, like many sea captains, preferred the company of his officers or the isolation of the chartroom on the bridge.

Captain Martin was proud of the *Florizel*; as far as he was concerned, she was superior to all other steamers of her size and build. He had been master of her for almost four years, and mate on her for two years before that. He had taken Newfoundland's first 500 volunteer soldiers across the Atlantic in the *Florizel* in October, 1914, and it had been heavy seas and head winds all the way. She had acquitted herself well, though her bells had sounded with every roll and the seas had buried her bow. The captain's expert seamanship had brought the *Florizel* through it safely.

Martin had good reason to be careful. As a member of the exclusive group of Newfoundland sea captains, he had never lost a ship or a man — but he had been witness to other disasters. In 1914 he had been the navigator on the S. S. *Stephano* when 77 men of the S. S. *Newfoundland** froze to death on the ice floes during the annual seal hunt. Captain Abram Kean, Commodore of Bowring's sealing fleet, and his two sons, Captain Joe Kean and Captain Westbury Kean, had been the central figures in that tragedy, and William Martin would not have been in their shoes for anything.

* See *Death on the Ice* by Cassie Brown, with Harold Horwood (Doubleday Canada Limited: Toronto, 1972).

But Fate decreed otherwise. Misfortune and anguish were heading his way.

Earlier on Saturday, Cook Fred Roberts fell asleep after dinner and found himself embroiled in a nightmare: the *Florizel* was on the rocks, screeching and jolting in the most terrifying manner; then the white, boiling seas were reaching for him. He felt the icy shock of water on his body and, with a strangled cry, sat bolt upright, heart pounding with terror, his body in a lather of sweat.

Hearing him, his mother called, "What's the matter, my son?"

Shaking because it had been so real, Fred replied, "I just had a dream that the *Florizel* was on the rocks and I barely escaped."

The good woman was not superstitious and had no concept of prescience, and she murmured, "It was just a dream, my son."

But it had been so real, so vivid to Roberts that at this moment the prospect of the voyage was anything but pleasant.

Third Officer Philip Jackman entered the kitchen where his wife Mary had just finished putting away the dinner dishes. He was a big, amiable young man with an engaging smile. He grinned now as Mary turned and saw him.

"Phil! What are you doing here?" she cried. "Aren't you sailing in a couple of hours?"

He told her that the departure had been postponed until seven-thirty: Mary did not ask why; she would not see her sailor-husband for another week or 10 days and was happy to have him with her for a few more hours.

Jackman had his customary after-dinner nap while Mary contentedly baked for the usual Saturday night game of cards at their house. Although Phil would not be there, she and her friends would have a lively game and wind up the evening with tea and sandwiches. They had no children, but they lived in a rented house with the owner, and Mary was never lonely.

After an early supper Phil kissed her goodbye. "The wind is in," he remarked as he stepped out the door. "It's going to be a rotten night."

Mary was a sailor's wife, but she knew little of the sea. However, after Phil had gone, it occurred to her that this was the first time he had ever passed a remark about the weather as he was leaving on a trip. She was not the type to worry unduly, but for some reason she could not put it out of her mind.

Because of the *Florizel's* delayed departure, Third Engineer Eric Collier also stayed home for supper. He said goodbye to his wife and two small children and hurried away. The southwest wind whistled through the bare branches of the trees and, unaccountably, Collier stopped, retraced his steps to his house, took his wife in his arms, and kissed her. He did not know why he had the urge to be so demonstrative, but he did. "Don't lock the door tonight," he said. "I wouldn't be surprised if we didn't sail."

In the comfortable boardinghouse of George and Dora Crocker, George and his friend, Joe Burry, both able-bodied seamen with the Red Cross Line, were having dinner before sailing. With departure already delayed once, there was speculation that the ship might not sail until the next day. But there was also the rumor among the crew that Mr. John Munn was anxious not to delay departure beyond 7:30 P.M. Crocker and Burry had to report aboard in the early afternoon.

There was a deep bond of friendship between Joe,

age 33, and 49-year-old George. Burry, unmarried, had come to St. John's from Greenspond some years before his friend, and had been readily accepted by the Red Cross Line. Crocker and his family had made it to the capital in 1912; he had found employment with Harvey's, owners of a fleet of freighters. Joe Burry had become a permanent boarder and was engaged to George's eldest daughter, Amy.

Harvey's laid off many of their men during the winter season when their fleet was laid up, but they put their best men to work in their factories at a reduced rate of pay until their ships went into operation in the spring. Crocker was one of those men. Captain Martin, always in need of reliable seamen when his regular crew had their time off, had heard about Crocker and asked him to join the *Florizel's* crew until such time as Harvey's needed him. George had accepted. This was to be his fourth and final trip; on his return, Harvey's would need him.

Now, as they ate, George winced every time he moved his arm. He was one of the crew who had been vaccinated when the *Florizel* arrived in port four days ago, and his arm was sore and inflamed.

"Maybe you should stay home," his wife Dora suggested.

But George laughed. "I'll be all right."

He was a thoughtful man. That morning he had chopped enough kindling for 10 days and stacked them neatly in the porch. "That'll hold you until I get back," he said.

Now dinner was finished. "Time to go," George said to Joe.

But they lingered. George made a fuss over his baby daughter, Dolly, and kissed Dora with great warmth. Joe, more reserved, was unexpectedly demonstrative with Amy.

The women were delighted with the unusual display of affection; the men did not seem to want to leave them, but at last they were going through the door. Still George returned. "I've got to kiss the baby again," he said.

He embraced his wife and Dolly. "Go on," Dora teased him, "it was *me* you really wanted to kiss."

George laughed.

It was the final goodbye. As the two men stepped out into the damp, raw afternoon, Dora called, "Look after him, Joe."

The Guzzwell family were saying goodbye to Billy. He was kissed and hugged in turn by his grandmother, his aunts, and his small cousins, Gladys and Lilly. They were his *real* family; they made up for the young mother he barely remembered.

Dressed in a new suit and wearing the warm woollen stockings with his initials W.G. woven in red into the band, knitted by his grandmother, he was so fair and handsome they were filled with pride as well as sorrow.

"I'll be back in a year and you won't know me. I'll be a real Yankee," he told them.

His Uncle Joe Moore eased him toward the door. "Come along, Billy, we have to go aboard," he said. Moore was second cook on the *Florizel*, and he had promised to deliver Billy to his mother in New York. "Time to go," he added. As one of the cooks he had to be aboard early enough to prepare dinner for the passengers.

There was one last flurry of farewells and they left.

CHAPTER 3

*MARINERS CONTENDED* that navigational aids were poor along the 57-mile stretch of coast from Cape Spear to Cape Race. At the extreme ends, Cape Spear and Cape Race had good lights and good fog horns; in between there were three very poor lights: one at Bull Head*, roughly 14 miles southward of Cape Spear; another at Ferryland Head, about 32 miles from the Cape. The third, at Bear Cove, some five miles beyond that, had an alternating light and a horn, which, mariners claimed, were of use only to small vessels and local woodsmen and were totally useless in thick weather.

The number of ships wrecked on this coast is legion and had rightly given it the name "Graveyard of the Atlantic." Seamen sailing southward often found their ships sagging in on the land, pushed by a strong inward current. In thick fog, vessels sailing confidently along the coast were frequently stranded on the shore. It was known that at times the surface of the Polar Current, inshore, reversed itself, setting in on the land and flowing northeastward, and those who were aware of this

* Referred to by mariners as Bay Bulls Light.

peculiarity took no chances; they would keep off land by 10 or 15 miles or more in threatening weather. Locally, seamen found that the Polar Current often set fairly well on to the shore just before a heavy gale of southwest wind.

*John W. Costello, lighthouse keeper at Ferryland Head, had that day noted that strings of slob ice pressing in on the shore appeared to be moving in an east or northeast direction, an indication that the tide was running against the powerful Polar Current.*

Captain William James, replacing Mate John Tucker, had signed on that morning and went on duty at 4:00 P.M. as first officer. Although the ship's barometer stood at 29.30, considered not a bad weather glass, he knew there was something brewing with the wind blowing from the southwest.

Departure was still 7:30 P.M., and engineers Thomas Lumsden and Herbert Taylor were supervising the stoking of the engine. Lumsden, as second engineer, was responsible for the engine while leaving and entering port. Once clear on the course, Taylor, as the fourth engineer (and stand-in for the chief engineer), would take over until midnight. The firemen and coal passers, 12 in all, were aboard and accounted for; they were all Spaniards, signed on in New York, good and willing workers. The rest of the crew, Fred Roberts and Joseph Moore among them, reported on board and the smooth-flowing work units readied the *Florizel* for her passengers.

They began to arrive, crowding the spacious social hall on the promenade deck with friends, relatives, and luggage as they lined up for their staterooms. John Munn had Room 1 to himself on the port side, amidships, immediately aft of the social hall. Sharing Room 2 were Major Michael Sullivan and John P. Kieley. Kieley was the owner of the Nickel Theatre. Others sharing the port staterooms were: George E. Stevenson, an American with Newfoundland business connections; F.C. Smythe, manager, the Woollen Mills; Alex Ledingham, marine engineer; Robert Wright, businessman; Patrick Laracy, owner of the Crescent Theatre; James Daley, buyer for a business firm; Edgar Froude, manager, Dicks and Company; C. H. Miller, representative of the U. S. Picture and Portrait Company; Thomas McMurdo McNeil, wealthy businessman and philanthropist; and James McCoubrey, an adventurous type of businessman who as a young man had spent four years in the Klondike panning for gold. Also on the port side were William Moore, Wilbert Butler, Michael O'Driscoll, William Earle, and the young volunteers, Fred Snow, Jack Parsons, Frank Chown, and Edward Berteau.

On the starboard alleyway, directly opposite her father, Betty Munn and her nurse, Evelyn Trenchard, settled in Room 18; and continuing aft along the alleyway were: George Moulton and his son Clarence, Arch Gardiner, George Parmiter, Mr. and Mrs. W. F. Butler, and Miss Mabel Barrett (still not aboard), who would share a room with blind Blanche Beaumont. Blanche was the niece of Stewardess Keough, who would also be in the same room.

Farther along were James Baggs, Mr. and Mrs. Massie and Katherine, Ralph Burnham, and Captain Joe Kean, who was on his way to Halifax to take command of the *Sable I* for the seal hunt. In the short cross-alleyway between John Munn and daughter Betty, Kitty Cantwell and Annie Dalton settled in Room 19.

Leading from the social hall on the promenade deck to the saloon deck was a great ornate stairway. From a landing the stairs branched to the port and starboard. At the bottom on either side, great swinging doors opened into the dining saloon.

The saloon and the first-class accommodations on

that deck were directly underneath the huge social hall, and a large, railed circular opening in the center of the hall permitted anyone above to observe the passengers dining, if they chose to do so. The circular opening was in a direct line with a huge skylight on the boat deck which was covered at night in compliance with wartime blackout regulations.

Occupying the first-class rooms forward of the saloon were John Connolly, butcher, who was taking his father, Michael Connolly, to Canada for medical treatment. The old gentleman was in the care of William Parmiter. W. E. Bishop, merchant of Burin also prominent in the herring fishery, Newman Sellars, and Gerald St. John occupied the other rooms on the starboard side.

Captain O. P. Belleveau and Noah Dauphinee shared Room 29 on the port side. Other passengers on this side of the ship were Minnie Denief and Elizabeth Pelley in Room 26 and Joseph, Mary, and baby John Maloney in Room 28. The chief steward's office was across from Room 26, next to the dining saloon.

The second-class accommodations were amidships on the port side and in the stern. Crew accommodation was on the starboard side amidships and under the forecastle head. The second-class passengers settled aft. Albert Fagan and R. J. Fowlow shared Room 38. Dave Griffiths (still not aboard) would share Room 37 with William Dodd. James Crockwell and Gregory Maloney shared a room in the stern; so did Puddester and Lynch. Billy Guzzwell had a room in the same area.

John Cleary, Paddy J. Fitzpatrick, Andy Power, and Jack T. Sparrow of Argentia, Placentia Bay, had fished out of Gloucester, Massachusetts, for six years. Paddy was a naturalized American citizen, but the others were not, though Paddy and John Cleary had been dory mates for years. All were returning to Gloucester to continue fishing.

Passengers and visitors gathered in the social hall. Farewell parties were in progress and there was much laughter and excitement. Those who had not been aboard before admired the elegant furnishings; they looked down through the great round opening to the snowy tables gleaming with silverware, already being set up for dinner. A large bookcase filled with contemporary novels stood in the center of the social hall; a piano, firmly anchored to the floor, was placed against the railing that surrounded the great stairway. Tables, chairs, and luxurious sofas filled the hall.

Many of the male first-class passengers were already settling down in the smoking room aft on the boat deck. It was equally luxurious, finished in mahogany and leather, with its own bar and buffet. Here, in complete privacy, they could smoke, drink, and play cards for as long as they liked. To get to the smoker, passengers had to step outside on the boat deck aft. The smoker had two doors; one opened aft, the other opened on the port side.

In the bustle of settling in, the waiters helped passengers stow their luggage. Henry Dodd recognized a former employer, William Butler and Mrs. Butler; greeting them warmly, he helped them to Room 15. Butler carried a little black bag and was careful to handle it himself while Dodd stowed the rest of the baggage.

John Johnston, pantry waiter, saw a familiar face in the crowd of jostling people. "Hello, Mr. Denief, are you going away?" he asked.

Denief said no. "It's my daughter Minnie who's going to New York." He formally introduced them.

Minnie, a slender young woman with an abundance of thick black hair under a modish hat, peered nearsightedly at Johnston through thick-lensed glasses. Johnston, she noted, was a cheerful, plumpish young man of medium height.

"Would you keep an eye on Minnie on the trip?"

Denief asked Johnston. "She's never traveled before."

Johnston promised he would, though in truth he had nothing whatever to do with passengers; his duties were confined to the kitchen and pantry.

Minnie was shown to her room where another woman was already settling in. Elizabeth Pelley, 33, was as composed and sure of herself as Minnie was unsure. Soon Minnie's father left. There were no lingering goodbyes in the dark, chill February evening, only anxious admonitions from Mr. Denief for Minnie to be careful, to look after herself, and to write as soon as she arrived in New York.

Minnie and Elizabeth liked each other at once. Neither had traveled before, and they derived comfort from each other's inexperience. Elizabeth told Minnie that she was going to live in New York with a minister and his family, and Minnie confided that she was going to New York to live with her sister.

Dinner was announced at six o'clock by a bugle. Waiter Jimmy Dwyer sent the clarion call throughout the ship, and the passengers came eagerly; dinner was the highlight of every voyage.

Minnie and Elizabeth were seated with the Maloney family, who had a stateroom next to theirs. Soon they were all quite friendly. Maloney and his family were on their way to Philadelphia and a new life. "I've got relatives there and they want us to stay with them," he said.

The two women confessed that they had never been away from home before, and Maloney added, gallantly, "When the ship docks in Halifax we'll take you on a tour and show you the sights."

The waiters pressed more food upon them, but Minnie ate sparingly, her stomach fluttering nervously at the merest hint of motion from the ship. She knew by the queasiness assailing her that she would be a victim of seasickness as soon as they sailed.

The dinner tables had been cleared at seven o'clock when a young man appeared looking for something to eat. It was Dave Griffiths. He had arrived in St. John's late in the afternoon and had had to tramp the streets looking for a doctor to vaccinate him. He had finally found one, and had barely made it aboard before sailing time.

"You're too late for dinner," the waiter told him, "but I'll find something."

At that moment a young woman arrived. "I was a little rushed and didn't have time to eat," she apologized. "Can I get something to eat now?"

She was very beautiful, blonde, and dressed in the height of fashion. The waiter hurriedly pulled out a chair for her next to Dave. "Sit down, Miss, I'll see what I can find," he said.

She introduced herself to her companion as Mabel Barrett, going to New York for an indefinite time. "Where are you from?" she asked.

He told her and they exchanged pleasantries. The waiter returned with biscuits, cheese, tea, and cookies, and the two young people dawdled over the food. They made a handsome couple, and the attraction seemed mutual.

The storm continued its northward trend, dumping snow and rain on Nova Scotia and Prince Edward Island. The perimeter arched along the south coast of Newfoundland, where snow was beginning to fly. Heavy swells were pounding that coast, but north of Cape Race they were less steep, rolling along the coast with the lie of the land.

The baby was asleep, supper was finished and the dishes washed, and Dora Crocker, vaguely restless, moved about the kitchen. Her daughters were upstairs preparing to go shopping and the house was very quiet.

Suddenly a brilliant flash of light drew her to the kitchen window and, before her eyes, a ball of fire* seemed to drift downward into their back yard, right over the spot where George always made the splits. She could clearly see the old wood block, hacked and splintered, before the light fizzled out.

She blinked. Had she really seen a ball of fire?

Dora was an outport woman, steeped in folklore. All her life she had heard stories of signs and tokens and discounted them utterly, but she called to Lucy and Amy. Had they seen the ball of fire?

They had not.

Dora did not lightly dismiss the phenomenon; neither did she dwell on it. If the girls had not seen it, then they had missed something unusual, but that was the end of it.

Presently Amy and Lucy were ready to leave the house, and Dora had the urge to get outside the four walls. "I'll go with you," she said.

The three of them walked along Water Street. Shop windows emitted a misty light, shoppers loomed mysteriously out of the gloom, to disappear just as mysteriously. If the girls showed any inclination to linger at the shop windows, Dora hustled them along until they were in the east end of the town and close to the cove where the *Florizel* berthed.

"Let's go see if the *Florizel* is gone," she said.

The girls did not protest, although they had learned, since living in St. John's, that it was not customary for women to approach the waterfront. They turned into the cove and the damp, raw wind stung their faces.

The *Florizel*, with only her navigation lights glowing, was just slipping away from the wharf.

* As told to the author by the Crocker family. There was no official report of a ball of fire.

PART II


# The Voyage
# According to
# The Enquiry

CHAPTER 4

AT 7:30 P.M. the order "Full Astern!" was piped down to the engine room. Blowing her whistle, the *Florizel* backed away from the wharf into midstream, a dark, hulking shadow, with all portholes, windows, and skylights covered and only her navigation lights showing against the great bulk of the Southside Hills that formed a rampart against the Atlantic. She was soon steaming out through The Narrows, her automatic whistle sounding frequently, warning all to make way.

Thus the *Florizel* began her last voyage, into the pages of history.

Because of the wind direction, the sonorous tones of her whistle hung over the town, each blast sounding for eight seconds exactly. The townspeople paused in their activities and gave her their full attention, listening intently as the blasts gradually faded, straining to catch the last lonely sound. Many would later recall that a strange, unsettled feeling came over them after she had gone.

Mary Jackman was listening, and to her it was a desolate, plaintive sound that touched a responsive chord. She listened uneasily as Mrs. Drover set up the card table, and murmured, "What's wrong with the *Florizel* tonight? She's making an awful racket."

*33*

Long after the *Florizel* had gone beyond her hearing, the sound of the whistle haunted her. She gave herself a mental shake and tried to dismiss it from her mind, but she could not.

Regardless of storm signals and warnings in the newspapers that the Toronto Weather Bureau was forecasting a gale with winds going around to the northeast, the barometer reading of 29.90 satisfied Captain Martin that it would be nothing the *Florizel* could not handle. His was an aneroid, a low-set barometer that registered at 29.60. It was less accurate than the mercury barometer, which registered at 30, but it was, in his opinion, a fine weather glass. The Toronto forecast had been inaccurate often enough for him to view this one with some skepticism. Weather patterns frequently changed by the time they reached Newfoundland; his own barometer, in which he put more trust, had been steady all day. Besides, if and when the wind backed to the northeast early Sunday morning, it would be a favorable one for the *Florizel* on her way to Halifax.

At 8:00 P.M. Fort Amherst was abeam on the southern point of The Narrows, and the *Florizel* steered for Cape Spear on a southeast-half-south course, at a speed of eight knots while her engine-room crew cleaned the stokehold. The ashes of the coals she had burned coming to port on her last voyage littered the stokehold, and during this period half of her steam was channeled to the ejectors, expelling the ashes into the sea. In fact, at the beginning of every four-hour watch she would automatically lose speed while her steam was used to eject the ashes of the coals she had burned during the preceding watch.

In New York on the previous trip, the *Florizel's* summer propeller had been replaced by a new steel winter propeller, and once the stokehold was cleaned, full steam would be directed to the engine and her speed would be 11 to 12 knots.

She was steaming along in clear water and Captain Martin, standing on the starboard wing of the bridge, ordered the log to be brought out. The log was the apparatus used to measure the speed of the ship as it streamed in her wake. The number of revolutions of the log was transmitted to a registering machine in the stern by means of a line that revolved with the log.

Philip Jackman, who was on the first watch, got the log from the chartroom and was about to pass it to the seaman, who would drop it over the stern, when the captain called, "Never mind, we can't use the log, we're in the ice." They were steaming through mushy, snowy sish* ice, two to three inches in thickness, the captain estimated; thick enough to keep the seas quiet but not thick enough to impede the *Florizel's* speed. However, the ice would sever the log line within minutes and it would be lost. Until they were in clear water they had no means of knowing the speed of the ship except by studying the sea from the bridge and estimating what she might be doing.

Although the moon was obscured, it was a bright enough night, but hazy; a slight swell heaving from the southeast sent her rolling with a long, slow cant from port to starboard and back again. It was the kind of motion that would eventually cause many of the passengers acute discomfort and misery.

As part of her wartime complement the *Florizel* carried two Naval Reservists to do gun duty in case of attack — not as unlikely as it sounded since the S. S. *Stephano*, sister ship to the *Florizel*, had been torpedoed† and sunk off Nantucket in October, 1916. Indeed, the *Florizel* might have been lost at the same time if she had not

* Ice the consistency of porridge.

† Without loss of life. The passengers and crew had been permitted to leave before she was torpedoed.

been behind schedule, for it was later reported that the torpedoing took place in the designated spot where the ships usually passed each other off the Nantucket Lightship.

So the *Florizel's* jolly boat, which could carry 24 persons, had been removed to make way for the big gun on her stern. She still carried six lifeboats, each with room for 42 persons. Number 3 on the port side was constructed of steel. Two Britishers, Alfred T. Hatchard and George Henry Curtis, manned the gun all day, but Hatchard and Curtis took regular watches at night like other sailors: not because they were forced to do so, but because they wanted to do so. It meant an extra 45 dollars a month. Curtis took the first watch.

For the passengers, the excitement of leaving port gradually waned, and they gathered in the social hall or the smoker. Kitty Cantwell and Annie Dalton, more adventurous than the other female passengers, dressed warmly and ventured outside on the promenade deck to watch the glimmering lights of St. John's. The raw southwest wind moaned along the deck as they watched the lights diminish to a glow; beneath their feet the deck reverberated to the steady pounding of the ship's engines, and the disembodied voices of the seamen came to their ears.

Annie watched the fading glow. Perhaps her thoughts were sad, perhaps she was thinking of the good friends she was leaving behind; two nights before, her closest friends had gathered to give her a farewell party. Would she ever see them again?

"Goodbye, St. John's," she said.

Kitty echoed, "Goodbye, St. John's."

A burly form loomed out of the darkness and a deep voice called, "Is that you, Kitty?"

Recognizing his voice, she replied instantly, "Yes, is that you, Bill?"

It was Quartermaster William Molloy, age 29, formerly a fisherman from Cape Broyle on the southern shore, along which they would presently be steaming. During his shore leave he boarded with Kitty's aunt and Kitty knew him well.

"You girls better get inside, we're battening her down."

Molloy went about his business, and the two women lingered for a few more minutes, leaning against the rail, letting the wind whip their faces, exulting in the motion of the ship. They were really on their way; excitement and adventure awaited them in the great city of New York!

The wind gusted and Annie shivered. "We'd better go inside."

Dave Griffiths and Mabel Barrett were still absorbed in each other, but as the ship gave the first long, slow roll, Dave knew that for the time being all thought of romance was at an end, because he was going to be sick and there was no time for niceties. A greenish pallor tinged his face and he rose abruptly. "I'm afraid I have to go."

Mabel nodded understandingly.

"I'll see you later, before we get to New York?" he asked.

"All right," she replied.

They parted, she to make her way up to the social hall and her stateroom on the promenade deck, Dave to bolt to his room aft of the dining saloon, where he was violently ill. His companion, William Dodd, sympathetically ministered to his needs.

The majority of passengers had gathered in the social hall. The bar had opened and the party atmosphere continued; the slow rolling of the ship, the staggering, hesitant movements of the passengers added to the general merriment. Full of confidence and good spirits, the young men grouped noisily together; there was good-natured ribaldry and bursts of laughter as they compared good times. Presently one of them sat at the piano and began to play, "It's a Long Way to Tipperary." Immediately, others drifted to the piano and the lusty sound of voices rang through the hall.

Maloney, the returned soldier, listened silently to the young men who were so lightheartedly going off to war. His own carefree youth had been lost in the Battle of Gallipoli.

Minnie Denief rose, her face ashen. "I've got to go to my room," she muttered, lurching toward the great stairway. Against the warnings of her stomach, she had lingered too long; the rolling of the ship had done its worst, she was going to be seasick. She weaved down the stairs, clutching the railing.

Elizabeth Pelley was suddenly beside her. "Are you all right?"

Minnie gasped, "I've got to lie down."

They made it to the room and Minnie collapsed on the lower berth. Elizabeth did the practical thing: she took off her clothes, put on her nightdress, and got into her berth. "Better get undressed and go to bed," she advised. "If you can get to sleep it won't bother you."

It seemed a wise decision. Minnie sat up shakily, removed her dress, corset, shoes, and stockings, but fell on the berth prostrate, violently seasick before she could undress fully. From the top berth, Elizabeth Pelley clucked sympathetically, then closed her eyes and ears.

The ash ejectors were working full blast as the *Florizel* steamed toward Cape Spear at about eight knots. John Shannon Munn and Captain Joe Kean were strolling the deck in spite of the chill wind. Both men knew the ship from stem to stern — Munn as the aristocratic managing director of the Red Cross Line and Kean as a sea captain who had sailed her many times to the seal hunt. Now, in the course of their walk around the deck, they came upon Mate William James.

"Goodnight," James said.

They returned his greeting and stopped for a moment. "We're in for weather again, I fear," Munn said.

"Looks like it, Mr. Munn," James agreed.

"But it'll be a short blow," Joe Kean said. "The wind will come around to the northeast quickly, and we'll have a fair trip to Halifax."

Munn nodded. "That's what we're looking for."

With this exchange of opinions, James moved on about his duties and soon John Munn and Joe Kean entered the comfortable smoker. It was filled with passengers enjoying the exclusiveness of all-male company. The bar was doing a fine business; already the roof ventilator was overtaxed as cigar smoke hung over the tables like a pall. Poker chips were out, and one of the topics of conversation was the "moving pictures" business, with John Kieley and Patrick Laracy holding forth on the merits of this wonderful invention. Major Sullivan, Thomas McNeil, Robert Wright, James Baggs, George Massie, James McCoubrey, Captain Belleveau, and Noah Dauphinee were among the passengers there, all enjoying each other's company. The voyage was off to an excellent start.

Meanwhile, Mate James, Second Officer John King, and Quartermaster Molloy had made sure that everything topside was securely lashed, and James and King reported to the bridge that all was under control. Then James, off duty now, went below to the chief engineer's room for a few minutes' social relaxation. Molloy went on duty on the bridge; King wrote up his log, then turned in. He had the midnight to 4:00 A.M. watch.

John Valder Reader had been an engineer with the Red Cross Line for 25 years, and had been chief engineer of the *Florizel* for the last eight years. He was an old friend of James and received him warmly. A tall, handsome Scot, Reader was absolute king in the engine room. Passenger Alex Ledingham was already in Reader's room, and they settled down for a chat. Presently Second Engineer Thomas Lumsden joined them, reporting to Reader that the ashes in the stokehold had been ejected and the *Florizel* would be gathering speed as she built up steam.

The *Florizel* passed Cape Spear and kept on steaming until the cape bore west by south, an estimated one and a half to two miles at 8:30 P.M. Taking a bearing by Cape Spear light, Captain Martin altered course to southwest, then 10 minutes later altered to southwest-quarter-south, allowing a quarter point to make a good southwest course to offset the possibility of an indraft* setting in on the cape, which might nudge her shoreward. Once around Cape Spear, she had the powerful Polar Current that swept along Newfoundland's northeast coast. The official speed of the Polar Current was from one to one and a half knots and was always of assistance to ships steaming southward to Cape Race, although with a northeast wind Captain Martin found it had a speed of from one and a half to two knots.

*Most Newfoundland mariners believed in "giving danger a wide berth" and sailed out into the Atlantic beyond Cape Spear for several miles before turning southward when bad-weather signs were so evident. Captain Martin ignored the warning signals and steamed along the shore on his regular fine-weather course, less than two miles offshore.*

To the starboard, through the thickening haze, Captain Martin could see the dark bulk of Motion Head, a distance of six to seven miles along the coast. The wind was freshening; it had backed from the southwest to the south-southwest since they had left port, and was hit-

* An inward flow or current.

ting the *Florizel* about a point on the starboard bow. A swell was running dead on her bow, causing the ship to plunge a little. The swells were not heavy, and the sish ice kept them from breaking. Although the wind and the sea were against her, Captain Martin was confident that the Polar Current would offset any hindrance from that direction. By one o'clock she would be round Cape Race and well on her way to Halifax.

The throb of her engine reverberated throughout the ship, but she was not moving any faster. With her ashes ejected and the Polar Current to carry her along, Martin had fully expected the *Florizel* to pick up speed quickly, but this had not happened. He paced the bridge from one side to the other, and Philip Jackman did the same. In the darkness they could see only the ice that rubbed against the ship's sides, but they knew it was possible for such an icefield to extend 50 miles or more from land.

Depending on the depth of it, sish ice could be a blessing or a curse. A moderately high wind and sea pressing for any length of time on the land could force the ice to pack and thicken enough to stop a ship dead. In fact, it had been known to extend solidly to the floor of the ocean close to shore and imprison a ship until a change of wind or tide carried it away. Tonight the sish ice was a blessing: a light scum just thick enough to keep the swells from breaking.

The wind was freshening, gusting occasionally. Martin continued to pace the bridge. Presently, he spoke to his third officer: "What do you think she's doing, Jackman?"

Jackman stared at the ice hissing by before giving an estimate. "I'd allow eight knots, Cap'n."

"Yes," Martin agreed reluctantly, "that's what I allow."

He moved to the bridge telegraph in the wheelhouse. It was still set at "Full Speed," which meant that by now she should have been doing anywhere from nine to 10 knots at least. "I'm going to the Chief's room for a few minutes," he told Jackman.

Martin was not worried. It was a practice of his to drop in on the chief engineer after leaving port. It was partly a social call, partly business; perhaps Reader would have something special to report about the engine.

Seafarers, referring to authority between bridge and engine room, say that "oil and water do not mix." The captain was the absolute authority on the ship and the chief engineer was accountable to him, but it was an area where the bridge trod softly. Engineers were a breed apart; their salaries were higher than those of any other crew member except the captain. When it came to the operation of the ship's engine, *their superior was the chief engineer, not the captain or the officer on the bridge*. In this respect the *Florizel* was no exception, although her bridge and her engine room worked in harmony.

Chief Engineer Reader was a highly skilled, thoroughly competent man who knew his job, and no captain, no officer of the watch, would dream of interfering. Officially, the chief engineer reported the engine room activities to the bridge at noon every day; only in emergency was there any deviation from this procedure.

If the ship was a little laggard on her course during the first couple of watches at sea, there were many possible factors involved, including a hung-over engine room crew whose pounding heads matched the pounding of the ship's engine. The firemen and the coal-passers quite often were physically unable to function as they should, and it took a couple of watches for them to straighten out. Perhaps at this time Captain Martin may have borne this in mind. No amount of carping would change the situation; it was a fact of life and one had to live and work with it.

42

With practiced skill, Captain Martin walked along the canting deck to the rear of the superstructure, opened the starboard door that led to the officers' quarters below, and entered. Reader would tell him now if there was any reason for the slow speed of the ship: if there had to be temporary easing up on a certain part of the machinery or if he had received last-minute orders to conserve coal. It happened occasionally that orders to economize with coal were passed directly to the chief engineer if the captain happened to be elsewhere on business at the time the orders were given. The slower the speed of the ship, the less coal she burned.

He tapped on the Chief's door, and Reader called, "Come in."

Martin entered, greeted everyone, and after a moment asked, "Is everything going all right below, Chief?"

"Everything okay below, Cap'n," Reader replied.

Martin was satisfied. He courteously remained with the group for about 15 minutes, then returned to the bridge. It was dark and hazy, the wind gusted as it swept around the bridge and sang in the rigging; dirty weather was not too far off.

Jackman was still pacing from port to starboard. Martin scrutinized the coast. Motion Head, the southern bulwark of Petty Harbour Bay, loomed murkily in the distance. The current here could insidiously sweep the *Florizel* inshore, and many a ship had come to an untimely end on the rocks there when her captain thought she was safely offshore. Some years back Martin himself had been aboard a ship that barely escaped. Now, observing Motion Head, he decided that his ship was sagging slightly landward as she crossed the mouth of the bay.

He drew Jackman's attention to it. "Keep her out. Don't let her go to the west *whatever*. If anything, let her make to the south."

Jackman passed the order to the wheelsman.

With the exception of her speed, all was well; the wheelsman and the lookout men were attending to business, and Martin decided to relax in his cabin. Their next checkpoint would be the Bay Bulls light, roughly 14 miles along the coast from Cape Spear. "We'll take a four-point bearing from Bay Bulls light as soon as we get on it," he told Jackman.

"Yes, Cap'n."

"I'm going to my cabin. Watch her, Jackman. Don't let her go 'in' any," he warned again.

"I'll watch her, Cap'n."

Martin moved to the steel ladder. "If you need me, give a toot of the whistle," he ordered.

His cabin and that of the first and second officers were immediately beneath the bridge; they were, in fact, part of the structure of the bridge, so that these officers were never more than a dozen or so steps from their official post. The officers' cabins faced aft and were not as large as his own, which faced forward, normally giving him an unrestricted view of the ship's progress.

He swung down the ladder and entered his cabin, picked up the newspaper, and settled down for a good reading session. The engine thumped steadily beneath him, there was power in the roll of the ship as she slid easily through the ice, her new steel propeller blades threshing through the sea. Normally it was a four-to-five-hour trip from Cape Spear to Cape Race, but allowing for the fact that she had not picked up speed, he had already decided to give her an extra hour or so to the cape. He now estimated that they would be up to Cape Race by 3:00 A.M. at the latest.

CHAPTER **5**

THE FLORIZEL'S speed did not increase. She rolled considerably, and her passengers were miserably aware of it.

In Room 16, Archibald Gardiner, formerly a reporter with *The Evening Telegram*, but suffering from indifferent health for some time, prepared for an early night to bed. He was feeling rotten and the berth looked inviting. His roommate, George Parmiter, had not put in an appearance as yet.

Steward Charlie Reelis knocked and entered. "Goodnight, Mr. Gardiner," he said cheerily. "Terrible weather we're having."

Gardiner agreed.

Reelis pointed to the rack over the settee. "Just in case you need it, there's your lifebelt, sir."

There were two lifebelts atop the rack within easy reach, and Gardiner nodded.

Reelis joked, "I don't think you'll need them this trip, sir."

Gardiner hoped not.

In a few minutes the steward left and Gardiner began to undress. The ship's motion was turning his stomach upside down and he had not fully undressed before seasickness overtook him. Still partially clothed, he crawled miserably into his berth.

There were still many passengers in the social hall since it was airy and comfortable in comparison to the closeness of the staterooms. A young man was still playing the piano, sitting ludicrously upright as the piano tilted first one way, then the other when the ship canted. His friends clustered around, bracing themselves against the piano or the lounges, their voices ringing lustily. Little Betty Munn, excited by the strange surroundings, peered out of her stateroom in wide-eyed curiosity toward the sound of singing and laughter. She was hugging a teddy bear.

Kitty Cantwell and Annie Dalton, peeking in through the social hall, wiggled their fingers in greeting at the blonde, blue-eyed child. "Hello there," Kitty said.

Betty, giggling delightedly, waved back at her.

The young women were too shy to intrude on the male party in the social hall. They returned to their room to unpack, chattering about their boyfriends and admiring each other's clothes. Annie had many boyfriends. Kitty was already spoken for; she would be marrying Mike McDonald in the autumn, but right now he had to take second place to this long-anticipated trip to New York. "I can't *wait* to get there," she said for the hundredth time.

"Hang up your clothes, Kitty, or they'll get wrinkled," Annie told her.

Kitty picked up a beautiful plaid suit Annie had made for her, hanging it in the wardrobe with great care. "Everybody will admire me when I wear this," she said blissfully, visualizing herself the object of admiring eyes as she strolled the streets of New York.

They finished unpacking, stowed their suitcases beneath the berth and the settee, and prepared for bed. It was still early, too early to think of sleep, impossible to think of sleep as far as Kitty was concerned. She unwound her long blonde hair and let it fall below her shoulders, brushing vigorously. Annie did the same with her long dark hair.

There was a brisk tapping on the door and Gordon Ivany, in spotless white jacket, stepped inside. "Good evening, ladies. Everything all right?"

"Oh yes," Kitty replied, "everything's fine."

He gave a cursory look around, shoved their luggage more snugly into place, then asked, "Is this your first voyage?"

They told him that it was.

"Then I must show you your lifebelts. There are two on the rack." He pointed to the rack over the settee. "We have to tell our passengers where they are in case of any emergency."

He gave another brief look around, satisfied himself that all was in order and left with a cheery, "Goodnight. Ring if you need anything."

"Goodnight," the girls echoed. The idea of an emergency had not registered at all.

The weather continued to deteriorate. The haze had thickened perceptibly, obscuring the land. The coastline from Cape Spear to Cape Race was precipitous and dangerous, looming over the sea and making it a very dark stretch of coast. Tonight it was blacker than usual.

On the bridge, Jackman became more alert, looking for landmarks that would show him the progress they were making, but he could distinguish nothing: the coast was a murky bulk, slightly blacker than the blackness of the night. With no log streaming, there was no way he could know for sure at what speed they were traveling. He did know the ship was still lagging.

He paced the bridge uneasily, eyes raking the night. The wind was rising and backing to the southward and was blowing dead on her bow; the ice, propelled by the wind and sea, was pressing against her. It was a combination he did not like, particularly along this shore. Suddenly he felt uncomfortable; his nostrils twitched; he had the distinct impression that the land to the west was looming closer.

Was the *Florizel* sagging into Petty Harbour Bay?

*Were they off course?*

He strode to the wheelhouse, checked the compass, and found it was still southwest-quarter-south. He told Molloy, "Don't let her go *anything* to the west. Keep her southward."

Still on tenterhooks, Jackman returned to the starboard wing and did not breathe a sigh of relief until Motion Head was abeam and they were beyond the currents sweeping into the bay. Landmarks were still indistinguishable but the bulk of the headland was unmistakable. He checked his watch; it was 9:30 P.M. Judging the distance from Cape Spear to Motion Head, which was roughly six to seven miles, he estimated that the *Florizel* was still doing only about eight knots. At 9:45 P.M. Motion Head was aft abeam,* and Bay Bulls light was a tiny pinprick about six to seven miles along the coast. Jackman watched the light but took no bearing; orders had been to take a four-point bearing, which would be when the light was directly on her beam, to the west.

The haze deepened. The wind, hitting the bridge squarely, carried the threat of snow.

Slowly the *Florizel* drew closer to the faintly glimmering Bay Bulls light. It was getting up to ten o'clock and the light was bearing about west by south, three points on her bow, when the first specks of snow drifted out of the night. Within minutes the flakes thickened and the light disappeared. Through narrowed eyes Jackman stared in its direction. Visibility was still up to a mile, he reckoned, but although he stared until his eyeballs ached he saw no further glimmer of it. It was obvious

* Between the middle and the stern of the ship's side.

that the weather had closed in and he was not going to get that four-point bearing. He did as he was ordered and gave a toot of the whistle.

In his cabin directly beneath the bridge, Captain Martin had not completely relaxed; one part of his mind absorbed the news of the day as he read the newspaper; the other was fully aware of the threat of weather. He had frequently peered out of the square window to check on her progress, but had been unable to perceive anything through the black night. Now, hearing the whistle, he put down the paper, put on his coat and cap, and checked the barometer before stepping outside. It was dropping rapidly. This meant a storm of short duration, with some snow and possibly rain, certainly nothing to cause undue concern.

Outside, snow streaked out of the night, the raw wind was freshening and backing to the south.

"We're going to have it thick," Martin remarked to Jackman as he came to the bridge.

"I'm afraid so, Cap'n; we lost Bay Bulls light before we could get a bearing."

"Where was it when we lost it?"

"About three points on her bow, sir."

Martin scanned the coast. He could still see the black bulk of Motion Head about two to two and a half points abaft the beam, which put the *Florizel* roughly midway between Motion Head and the Bay Bulls light. She was still slow, but with the wheelsman favoring a southward course, she should be off the land by a good three miles.

Then Jackman told him, "Cap'n, I thought we were sagging into Petty Harbour Bay a little while back."

*According to the court records there is a discrepancy in the testimony relating to the "sagging in" on the land.* Captain Martin stated: "Jackman told me he thought she was sagging in Petty Harbour Bay a while back, but he

49

hauled her out a little to the south'ard."

The court asked, "To get her out of the bay and put her farther off shore?"

Martin replied, "Yes, he hauled her off perhaps a quarter or half point."

"How long did he keep her so?"

"Not very long because when I went up to the bridge she was clear of everything, and we were on the course I gave him," Martin answered.

In Jackman's testimony, he said, "I thought she was sagging in, but when we got Motion Head abeam, I was quite satisfied that she was not. I only *thought* she was sagging in."

The court asked, "Did you take any steps to correct this sagging in?"

"Yes, I went in the wheelhouse and told the man at the wheel to be careful over his course and to let her do nothing to the west," Jackman replied.

"Did you take any observation for this purpose of finding out whether she was sagging in or not?"

Jackman said, "There was no light or anything to take any observation from."

Martin assessed the situation. If the *Florizel* had sagged in on the land and there was no light to guide them, it was imperative that they try to establish how close she was to land. Ordinarily the sounding lead would indicate their position, but soundings along the southern shore, from Cape Spear to the south of Ferryland (roughly 30 miles), hardly varied at all on the normal course of the ship and, because of it, the lead was considered practically useless in thick weather. However, soundings would show if she was *inside* her course. He passed the order to Jackman: "Get the sounding lead."

The sounding apparatus consisted of a wire on a reel with lead weighing 28 pounds. The lead had a hollow bottom filled with soap, tallow, or grease, so that when it hit bottom, whatever was on the ocean floor adhered to it and gave mariners an idea what they were traveling over; it helped identify their position.

Connected to the line was a brass tube into which a chemically coated glass tube had to be inserted. When the apparatus plunged to the sea bed, the pressure of the water forced the chemical up inside the glass tube and indicated the depth of water they were steaming over. The *Florizel* carried about 60 sounding tubes.

Martin himself inserted a glass sounding tube in the brass tube. The apparatus was then passed to Seaman Dooley and Seaman Gover, who carried it aft where the sounding gear was located. It was 10:10 P.M.

Martin and Jackman, hypersensitive to the dropping of the atmospheric pressure, paced the bridge restlessly, stopping in the wings to stare at the ice along her side. They decided that it was not packing; in fact, it appeared to be very loose.

"What do you think she's doing now?" Martin asked.

"No more than eight knots, sir," Jackman estimated.

They were both puzzled as to why she had not picked up speed. Granted there was a swell on her bow and the wind was dead ahead, but neither wind nor swell was so strong as to hinder a ship like the *Florizel*.

*Each man harbored these thoughts, but neither spoke of them to the other, nor did they telephone the engine room to ask bluntly why her speed had not increased. Reader had said all was okay, and, as far as Martin was concerned, one did not question it.*

In about 10 minutes, Dooley and Gover returned with the sounding tube. "We ran out 160 fathoms of wire, sir, an' got a sandy bottom," Dooley reported to Jackman, who in turn passed the glass tube to the captain. Scaling the pressure tube, Martin duly noted 80 fathoms in his logbook and put the used tube in a reserve case in the chartroom. He was greatly relieved. The 80 fathoms put him where he thought they should be: about three miles offshore. "We're all right," he told Jackman, "but we can't be too careful."

They continued pacing. They were, Martin estimated, roughly a dozen miles along the coast from Cape Spear, the last point of departure taken more than an hour and a half ago; they were already behind schedule and likely to fall farther behind if the *Florizel* did not increase her speed.

The wind, backing to the south, gusted lightly, snow raked the deck, whirling around the bridge and through the ship's rigging. The swells were starting to heave from the southward, hitting her about a point on the port bow, and a nasty cross-sea was developing.

She steamed onward, her movements a little more abrupt as the swells caused the sea to chop. Martin and Jackman remained alert, checking on the binnacle occasionally to make sure she was on course, each time cautioning the wheelsman not to let her make anything to the westward.

The barometer was still dropping. Visibility had lessened to about half a mile.

Fourth Engineer Herbert Taylor, 21, was stand-in for the chief engineer. Theoretically, the first watch at sea was the chief engineer's watch, but the chief did not actually take a watch so this became the job of the fourth engineer in all ships. Steam pressure had fallen to 167 pounds while the ashes were being ejected, but under Taylor's watchful eye, the gauge had risen to the normal pressure of 175 pounds. The furnace roared, steam hissed, and the pistons danced; she had enough steam now to give her the 75 revolutions that could make her travel at 11 to 12 knots, *but she was still doing only eight knots.*

The storm veered to a more northerly track. It was severely buffeting Nova Scotia and western Newfoundland; snow clogged streets and highways, all transportation was paralyzed. St. John's and the southeast coast was more fortunate this time, being in the warmer southeasterly flow of wind, which was gusting up to 25 miles an hour. Soft, wet snow stuck like frosting to houses, street poles, and fences and quickly choked the streets. Fortunately, businesses had closed and few people were abroad.

The card game was going strong in the Jackman home, but Mary was playing a terrible game, much to Mrs. Drover's disgust. She said, annoyed, "What's got into you, Mary Jackman? You keep putting us in the hole."

Mary, flustered and apologetic, could only say, "It's that *Florizel*, she's on my mind tonight," adding ruefully, "I don't know why."

It was true. The forlorn sound of the ship's whistle still haunted her.

In the Crocker household, boarders were having their snack before going to bed. Dora, peering out the window at the blowing snow, said uneasily, "My, this is a stormy night for a ship to be at sea."

One of the men replied, "Don't you worry, Mrs. Crocker, nothing can hurt the *Florizel*."

They all had faith in the remarkable capabilities of the sturdy ship.

The *Florizel* now began to pitch and roll in the cross-sea, sending most of her passengers reeling to their cabins.

In Room 19, Kitty and Annie had finished their toilet and undressed, striving to maintain their balance as the ship's movements grew rougher. Kitty loved it; it added excitement to the very act of going to bed. Annie did not like it at all; her skin took on a pallor and she hastily

53

climbed the little ladder to the upper berth where she collapsed, groaning.

Kitty, who was not the least bit seasick and did not want to go to bed, was sympathetic: "Poor Annie! Never you mind, once we're around Cape Race it'll be easier going." She had always heard that, whatever the weather, it would be rough going around Cape Race.

Annie moaned again.

About 20 seasoned travelers were still in the smoker, unmindful of the increasing motion of the ship. There was no piano, but occasionally John Kieley burst into song. He had a mellow voice and was in a mellow mood as the drinks flowed. "I used to be a singer," he told the men as they applauded.

He explained that as a singer he had been a regular on the movie-theater circuit, and The Nickel had been one of the theaters in which he performed; when the owner retired he had been given the option to buy. He had bought the franchise, retired from the uncertainties of a singing career, and done exceptionally well in the years since. "I'm on my way to Montreal and New York to buy films for the spring and summer," he told them.

Life was good to John Kieley; he was successful and well-to-do and he loved life. In a benign, expansive mood, he ordered drinks all round.

Captain O. P. Belleveau and Mate Noah Dauphinee decided to turn in. They left the smoker and strolled around the boat deck, skirting the big engine-room skylight immediately to the fore of the smoker, their sailors' legs adjusting to the canting deck as they walked around the smokestack belching its black smoke. Soft, thick snow pelted against them, the wind rattled the lifeboats in the davits as they swung and creaked with the roll of the ship. The men were indifferent to the snow and the tilting deck; the steady thump of the engine was a comforting sound to their ears. Heads bent to the wind, they passed the dark bulk of the little Marconi house squatting in front of the smokestack, went past the covered bulk of the social hall skylight, and proceeded down the ladder leading down to the promenade deck.

"Once around the deck," Belleveau said, "and then we turn in."

Scuffling through patches of snow, they took a quick turn around the ship and then went straight downstairs to their stateroom. Theirs was an outside room with a porthole, which they left wide open.

The two undressed and went to bed.

It was getting on to eleven o'clock when Major Sullivan and Thomas McNeil decided to take a stroll on the promenade deck before turning in. The *Florizel* was rolling and pitching in a lively way, but Sullivan, tall, hefty, big-boned, was a seasoned traveler and had no great difficulty walking the deck; nor did McNeil. The wind whistled under the sheltered deck, snow stung their faces as they peered over the rail. The dim reflection cast by the ice itself as the sea rose and fell was sufficient for them to gauge the turbulence. "The ice is just thick enough to keep the sea from breaking," McNeil observed.

Sullivan agreed. It would probably be a much rougher voyage but for the sish ice, he said.

It was not the kind of night that invited loitering, and both men retired to their rooms on the port side of the promenade deck.

Major Sullivan, his bulk almost filling the stateroom, eyed the lower berth to which Kieley had laid claim by a scattering of personal articles. With the rolling and pitching, it was going to be an uncomfortable night all round; in the upper berth, it was going to be that much worse.

Sullivan did not hesitate. He removed Kieley's things, undressed, and crawled into the lower berth.

Philip Jackman, staring down at the heaving seas, could not delude himself that the *Florizel's* speed had increased. Beside him, Captain Martin's stocky figure was hunched over the starboard railing, eyes riveted to the ice.

Both men were more puzzled than ever. With the telegraph set at "Full Speed" it could not be assumed she was doing less. If she were doing less than full speed, Reader would have come to the bridge with an explanation.

Either the engine-room crew were not up to their best performance yet, or the sea, the wind, and the ice were holding her back.

At 11:00 P.M. the captain ordered another sounding, and again Dooley, this time with Quartermaster Molloy, threw the sounding tube over the stern. The wire rolled out and they reported back to Jackman: "Here you are, sir, 160 fathoms."

Captain Martin scaled the tube, which showed 85 fathoms of water; the lead indicated a sandy bottom.

Martin was satisfied. He was sure he knew where they were in spite of the thickness of the weather. The 85 fathoms put the *Florizel* seven to eight miles southward of his last sounding, roughly 20 miles along the coast from Cape Spear. On a course that favored a southerly helm, she had to be three to four miles offshore. They had lost a lot of time, but they were on course. "We're all right," he told Jackman. He was absolutely sure on that point.

The ship had still not increased speed when Martin ordered another sounding at 11:55 P.M. This time 170 fathoms of wire ran out, the lead showed a sandy and rocky bottom. Charting the soundings, Captain Martin concluded that they were steaming on the fine-weather course that he normally took. The coastline ran to the westward (magnetic west); his course was to the southward; so he was steadily steaming away from land and from any danger. He was, he estimated, another five to six miles farther along the coast, nearly up to Cape Broyle, roughly 30 miles from Cape Spear and 27 miles from Cape Race, his next checkpoint.

The barometer was still dropping, snow had decreased visibility to a quarter of a mile, and Captain Martin made a decision. Although the *Florizel* was taking a more southerly course, the wind was backing out to the southeast, hauling the seas around with it and creating great turbulence, and the shallow Bantems, fishing grounds of the southern shore fishermen, with a depth of only nine fathoms in certain areas, lay directly in her path. The heavy swells heaving in from the Atlantic would build steeply over the Bantems, creating dangerous seas that could break and cause the *Florizel* to founder. Even if the seas were not breaking, it would be decidedly unpleasant steaming over the Bantems tonight.

He decided to alter course and haul her out into the Atlantic, away from the Bantems.

The watch was changing at midnight when he gave the order: "Alter course to sou'-sou'west."

Second Officer John King was taking over the watch from Jackman when the order was given. "I don't like going over the Bantems with a swell heaving in like this," Martin told him; then to the wheelsman, Charles Bailey, who had taken over from Molloy, he ordered, "Don't give her anything to the westward, keep her *well* to the sou'-sou'west."

King approved the decision. "There's a lot of room outside the Bantems," he said.

There was the whole Atlantic Ocean.

# 6

*THE HEAVY* swells were beginning to "heave home" now with the force of the Atlantic behind them, and even with the sish ice to quiet them, they fell in tumbled confusion on top of each other. Laboring, the *Florizel* steamed on a south-southwest course that would take her away from the dangerous coast.

Seamen Charles Bailey and Thomas Green had relieved Dooley and Gover. Gunner Alfred Hatchard relieved Gunner George Henry Curtis.

It had been an uneventful watch for the chief Marconi operator, Cecil Sidney Carter; there had been no signals received, none sent. The government-owned Marconi station at Mount Pearl, a few miles inland from St. John's, had sent out a few signals but nothing relative to the *Florizel*. At two o'clock Carter would go off duty.

The Marconi room was tiny and cramped, about seven by eight feet. It was a steel structure with a wooden roof, and had been added after the ship had been built; but it had a bunk, a tiny settee, and a corner for the wireless apparatus. Its one luxury was a carpet. It was functional, and comfortable enough for one person.

Carter and his assistant, Bernard John Murphy, were actually employees of the American Marconi Company of New York, which owned the apparatus. Carter, being a bright young man, had rigged a private wire from the Marconi room to his own quarters, Room 21 on the promenade deck, thus eliminating all necessity of leaving the instruments unattended in any emergency. However, standing orders to his assistant were to call him on the private wire if any such emergency arose. In that event, Carter felt that he would have to take over.

The wireless was operated by current from the engine-room dynamo and its range was roughly 250 miles. Marconi had also supplied an auxiliary set, which had a range of 80 to 100 miles. The operators themselves took care of this set-up. The batteries had been fully charged during the night, and the test at 9:15 P.M. had found everything to be in top working condition.

In wartime it paid to be prepared.

Major Sullivan had slept soundly enough for an hour or so, but a noise at the edge of his consciousness awakened him; he lay there, foggily wondering what had sent sleep flying. The rolling and pitching were more pronounced now, and from outside the door there came a muttered curse.

The door swung inward and Kieley lurched into the cabin. He was far from sober and, seeing Sullivan in his berth, spoke with grave asperity: "You have taken my berth, Major Sullivan."

Sullivan grunted, heaved his bulk, and turned his back to Kieley.

Kieley, still civil and fairly respectful of the major's rank, was mildly indignant. "That is my berth, sir."

"Go to hell," Sullivan muttered.

Kieley was offended, "To hell with *you*," he said stiffly, and repeated it again, "To hell with you!"

He sat on the settee, muttering in annoyance as the ship pitched wildly. Sullivan's back was solid and uncompromising, and with one last "To hell with you!" Kieley undressed, maneuvered the short ladder to the upper berth, and tried to settle down to sleep. However, he lay uneasily, fearing that he might be projected across the stateroom as the ship labored onward.

It was, he decided, too dangerous to stay there. With great deliberation he eased down the ladder, glared at Sullivan's back, then dressed. Hauling out his suitcase from beneath the lower berth, he took out a bottle of whisky, gave Sullivan's back one more glare, muttered, "To hell with you," and headed back to the smoker.

The major was annoyed. Not only had Kieley awakened him, but he was pitching about the berth so that he became more alert and conscious of the laborious creaking of the ship. The longer he lay there, the more elusive sleep became. As spacious as the stateroom was (by shipboard standards), it was suddenly too close and airless for the big man, and with a sigh of exasperation, he, too, got up, dressed and left the stateroom. It was too late to visit with anyone, so he lurched aft, hauled himself up the stairway, eased out on deck, and slipped into the smoker.

Kieley and a handful of other passengers were engrossed in poker. If Kieley was aware of his presence, he ignored him magnificently. The bar had long since closed, but most men had their own private stock of whisky and were not in want. Captain Joe Kean had apparently been walking the deck; he came into the smoker immediately behind Sullivan, covered in snow. Removing his topcoat, he settled beside Sullivan to watch the game.

The *Florizel* was bouncing around and Sullivan remarked, "She's rolling hard tonight."

"She is that," Kean agreed, adding, "but she'd pitch

more if there was no ice to keep the sea down.

"There's no doubt about that," Sullivan said.

At midnight, Third Engineer Eric Collier relieved Herbert Taylor. The engine room vibrated with the powerful thumping of the machinery. Here was the heart of the ship, pulsing with the beat of life. The whole engine room was a great powerhouse, utterly remote from the windswept bridge, the cold outer reaches of the ship. It was almost unbearably hot; the bodies of the Spanish firemen glistened with sweat. The outside world, with its raw winds, did not exist for these men feeding the great muscle that gave life to the ship.

According to the blackboard, the boiler had built up to 175 pounds of pressure (nearly a full head of steam), but the engine had averaged only 69 revolutions a minute in the eight to midnight watch. It should have been averaging up to 75 revolutions.

Collier, checking the blackboard with this information chalked up, asked, "Everything going all right?"

Taylor said yes.

The firemen going off watch did not go to their quarters under the forecastle head; instead, they curled up in the corners of the warm stokehold and instantly went to sleep. It was not forbidden, and they did this frequently in the winter. The stokehold was not unbearably hot; heat from the roaring furnaces flowed up through the fiddley* above them and dissipated in the cold night air. Three flights of steel steps led from the stokehold to the boat deck through the fiddley.

The middle watch took over. Taylor, checking around the engine room, did not leave until 12:10 A.M.

As was usual, the stokehold had accumulated ashes

* The uppermost part of the stokehold. The roof of the fiddley is elevated above the main deck and is covered with a grating called the *fiddley opening* to provide ventilation.

of four hours' burning, and Collier gave the order to eject them. This would take up to half an hour, during which time the speed of the ship would drop by at least a knot.

At midnight the automatic electrical anemometer (wind gauge) at the meteorological station in St. John's was reporting winds up to 33 miles an hour.*

The *Florizel's* movements grew more lively as the sea and wind shifted around to the southeast. Laboring through the heavy cross-sea, she jumped and reeled as the swells careered in different directions. Jarred, jolted, and unable to run free, she corkscrewed onward, head pitching, stern lifting, partially exposing her propeller, causing her screw to race. In the engine room Collier had stationed himself by the throttle valve to "catch" her when she lifted, shutting her steam and cutting the engine when the propeller was above water. He did this so expertly that Captain Martin, on the bridge, was unaware of the racing.

On this course the *Florizel* was steaming out into the Atlantic, away from land, and it was not necessary to take any soundings.

The wind steadily freshened, singing around the bridge, rattling the lifeboats in the davits. When it gusted, the snow swept across the deck in blinding sheets, piling up in every corner and crevice. By 2:00 A.M. the wind had backed right out to the southeast on the *Florizel's* beam, and the sea had followed, so that the cross-sea gradually merged with the swells, which rolled dead on her port beam with the awesome force of a thousand miles of ocean behind them. Now she began to steam through small patches of open sea. The phos-

* On Beaufort's wind scale: Force 7, moderate gale.

phorescent glitter of cresting waves loomed here and there, a savage flicker of white.

Cape Spear recorded: February 24, 12:00 A.M. to 2:00 A.M., wind, a storm.

Southward of the icefield where seas were turbulent, Ferryland recorded: February 24, 2:00 A.M. Wind about south-southeast, a real storm with wet snow and rain. Terrible sea during the night.

Captain Martin's uneasy feeling grew stronger. Not because of the weather; the wind had reached only moderate gale force and would not affect the *Florizel* in the least. Nor did it worry him that she was on a lee shore in heavy seas; but her lack of speed continued to puzzle him, kept him prowling between bridge, chartroom, and his cabin. It was halfway through the second watch and her speed had not increased as he had expected; if anything, it had decreased, if he was any judge. "What do you think she's going now, Mr. King?" he asked the second officer.

King, staring over the side, estimated six to seven knots. Again, there was no conversation or speculation as to why she was steaming so slowly.

"Keep her steady on the sou'-sou'west course," Martin ordered the wheelsman, then went below to pace the deck outside his cabin.

The snow turned to a sleety rain, giving slightly better visibility that showed the occasional gleam of crests as the ship continued through more open patches of sea. Over she rolled, and quickly back to meet the onslaught of the following waves, but no seas boarded her.

About this time Captain Joe Kean and Major Sullivan left the smoker, Sullivan to return below and try to sleep, Captain Kean to take a stroll before turning in. He made it across the careening boat deck with a sailor's sure gait and found Captain Martin pacing to and fro outside his cabin.

They greeted each other. Martin was used to seamen who traveled as passengers turning up on deck at all hours of the night. Unable to sleep like ordinary people, they napped during the day and prowled the deck the rest of their time at sea, staring into the night, looking for lights and landmarks, unable to shuck off, for the briefest time, the habit of a lifetime, mentally sailing the ship as though they were the master. It was habit, and he was fully aware of it because that was the way *he* was aboard another man's ship. Joe Kean was a restless passenger.

They braced themselves against the canting deck, rain hissed by on the wind as the *Florizel* pitched onward, her flat-bottom bow thumping over the waves. "It's a nasty night, Cap," Martin said.

Joe replied, "Yes, it's a dirty night, all right." His eyes were raking the black night landward. "It's difficult to see the lights on the coast tonight."

Martin told him bluntly, "I'm not looking for lights tonight, Captain Kean, I altered course to sou'-sou'west at midnight. We're too far offshore to see any lights."

"Good!" Joe Kean said.

He lingered only briefly. "I think I'll turn in now. Goodnight."

"Goodnight," Martin replied, and watched the dark bulk of the man disappear into the sleety night. Then he continued his lonely vigil.

Cecil Sydney Carter in the Marconi house had been relieved by Bernard John Murphy, and was vainly trying to sleep. His quarters, Room 21, were directly at the foot of the stairway leading to the boat deck and the smoker. Another stairway, leading below to the second-class accommodations, was at the end of the starboard alleyway, also outside his door, and generally the passageway had a lot of traffic. There was little or none at this hour of the night, but the wild motion of the ship kept him awake.

In the engine room, Collier and Oiler Thomas Hennebury had taken turns to cut the racing engine before she "got away" from them; they had succeeded in catching her each time, and finally, at 2:30 A.M. when the cross-sea had merged with the swell, the racing had just about stopped, but it had brought her revolutions down and further decreased her speed. Lack of speed made her more vulnerable to the vagaries of the truculent sea. She still rolled and heaved alarmingly.

Passengers who had been too seasick to sleep now suffered from the violent jostling as they were tossed about in their berths. Kitty Cantwell was not seasick, but she certainly could not sleep with the incessant motion of the ship and Annie's continual moaning. "Never mind, Annie, it can't last much longer," she said comfortingly, adding, "I guess the Captain has taken us out into the Atlantic."

Annie gave a prolonged moan.

Incredibly, Elizabeth Pelley slept, but Minnie Denief lay awake and ill. She hated the berth, hated the room, and hated the ship; she wanted only to be back on land. To add to her misery, she could hear the wailing of the Maloneys' infant son in the room next door. God help Mary Maloney if she was seasick and had a sick baby too.

Alex Ledingham had been in his berth since half past nine, but he had slept lightly, waking fully as the ship's motion increased. His companion, Robert Wright, had gone to play poker and still had not returned.

As a marine engineer Ledingham was familiar with every sound of a ship's engine, and to his experienced ear the *Florizel's* engine was not working regularly to-night. The ship seemed to "lift" a little too.

He turned over, trying to sleep.

Again, Major Sullivan found it intolerably stuffy in his stateroom. John Kieley had not put in another appearance and sleep had not returned, as much as he tried to will it, and his annoyance grew as the motion of the ship added to his discomfort. Suddenly he could not stand the airless room another minute. Once more he got up, dressed, took a blanket from his berth, left the room and staggered into the social hall. Only a small night light was burning, casting a dim glow in its immediate vicinity. Beyond its range all was shadow and darkness, but it was cool and airy and a man could breathe at least.

Sullivan picked one of the comfortable sofas forward, lay down, and covered himself. He had to brace feet and shoulders against the lounge to keep from falling to the floor, but presently he began to drift into a light sleep.

The *Florizel* steamed onward, the swells marching against her port side, sending her keeling to starboard. She came back quickly, was lifted high on the crests, and dropped, laboring, into the deep troughs. The open patches of sea were more prevalent and the glimmer of wave-tops flickered in the dark. Rain, like ice needles, streaked by on the wind, bounced off the superstructure, and ran along the deck.

Captain Martin had returned to the bridge, pacing with Second Officer King. The barometer was still falling and the black night pressed around them. Puzzled as he was about the ship's lack of speed, Martin still did not question the engine room crew. He was confident that she was safely off the land; the sou'-sou'west course since midnight had taken the *Florizel* well outside the shallow waters of the Bantems, and except for the swell and the wind on her beam, which appeared to be slowing her, all was well. He was absolutely sure she was out into the deep Atlantic, so sure that he had not bothered to take any soundings after midnight.

Once before, the *Florizel* had made slow speed, and that had been coming across the Atlantic from the other side, loaded with munitions. She had run head on into a heavy gale of wind with mountainous seas running; she had pitched and rolled until her bells rang continually, and she buried her nose in spray. At that time, two years back, she had made only four knots; but tonight's weather could not compare to that terrible storm.

By 3:00 A.M. the barometer had dropped to 29.10; visibility had increased up to a mile, but Captain Martin, steaming away from land, was not looking for lights — he was not looking for anything.

Gunner Hatchard, on stand-by until 3:00 A.M., now returned for lookout duty on the starboard side of the bridge; Quartermaster Thomas Green was at the wheel.

It looked as if the *Florizel* was about to leave the safety of the sish ice; she was steaming through large patches of open water, and the white tops of heavy swells flickered on the black sea. On the periphery of Hatchard's vision, vagrant luminous impressions grabbed his attention, then she was steaming again through strings of ice.

It was shortly after three o'clock that Hatchard snapped to attention. *There! Abaft the beam! Had he seen a flash of light?* Not exactly a flash of light, but the reflection of a light is what it looked like. He stared until his eyeballs ached, but there was no following flash and he relaxed. What he had seen must have been the gleam of a cresting wave; it often happened at sea when a sailor's eyes played tricks on him.

*67*

Even as he settled this in his mind, King spoke up, "Captain, I believe I saw a light on the starboard quarter."

Martin said sharply, "A light? Are you sure?"

King was dubious. "No, not absolutely sure."

Straining to see through the rain-swept night, Martin and King stared over the starboard quarter. Hatchard, having overheard, also searched until his eyes watered with strain; if anything, the black night seemed to become more impenetrable.

King suggested, "It might have been a loom light."*

Martin squelched that. To see even the faintest loom of light on a night like this, they would have to be quite close to shore. He said, "I doubt if you saw a light, John; we're too far offshore."

King said, "It may be Bear Cove Head light."

*Bear Cove Head light!* The poorest light on that stretch of coast, so poor it was a standing joke among mariners. How could they have seen Bear Cove light when they were so far from land?

Martin was a careful man. He went to Hatchard. "Did *you* see a light?"

Hatchard replied cautiously, "I thought I saw a light, Cap'n."

"Why didn't you tell me?" Martin snapped.

"I didn't see it a second time, and I thought I was mistaken, sir."

"Where did you see it?"

"Abaft the beam, sir."

Martin scanned the thick, black night with binoculars, looking for a light or a ship, anything to explain why two men had seen what they thought was a light. Hatchard and King again tried to pierce the rain-streaked blackness, but there was no further sign, not

* Faint appearance of a light in the distance: to appear as on a mist.

even a faint illumination. After a prolonged look, Martin was satisfied that both men had made a mistake. "If there had been a light you would have seen it while it was abeam," he told them

They had come to the same conclusion.

By 3:30 A.M. they had steamed into clear water, and the sea, released from the confines of ice, crested and showed its teeth; swells with ugly white tops reared on the *Florizel's* beam, pitched her madly to starboard. In the staterooms, luggage began to slide and roll about the floors, wardroom doors crashed open and clothes danced wildly on hangers like puppet scarecrows. Passengers clutched the wooden sideboards of their berths to keep from being flung to the floor; a few were still wretchedly ill.

Kitty Cantwell did not get seasick, nor was she unduly concerned about the ship. Annie was her main concern; she looked frightful, her color was a pasty green, deep shadows had appeared under her eyes, she lay limp and pallid.

"You're all right, Annie," she soothed, hanging onto the sideboard. "We're well out in the Atlantic, and she's rolling with the waves," she said comfortingly, though in truth she did not know what she was talking about.

This time Annie did not even moan.

Alex Ledingham had slept poorly, if at all. His heavy seaman's trunk was sliding and scraping from one side of the room to the other, banging against the settee and the wall. His companion, Robert Wright, had finally returned from the poker game, undressed, and gotten quietly into bed. Ledingham did not know if he slept or not. Finally the sliding trunk was too much even for his nerves of steel. He got up, cornered it, and jammed it securely beneath the berth, then returned to bed. But sleep did not come.

The wind had not increased greatly, but the seas

heaving in from the Atlantic hit the *Florizel* broadside, exploded in a welter of spume, burying her port deck in solid sheets of spray, sending her canting to starboard, her boats swinging and squealing in the davits. Along the windward side, portholes began to leak freely, some more severely than others. Passengers discovered water dripping onto the floor.

Some of them dressed, staggered through the alley-ways, and negotiated the dining saloon, reeling and lurching from table to table. The chief steward was in his office immediately forward of the saloon, and he gave a sympathetic ear to their complaints. "We'll look after it right away," he soothed each in turn. Then he hurried through the laboring ship to the stewards' quarters, rousing them all, including his brother Henry. "Get mops and buckets; passengers are complaining about leaks in their rooms," he ordered, directing them to the rooms on the port side.

The stewards collected mops and buckets and headed for the flooded staterooms. Nobody was alarmed; it happened sometimes in unusually rough sea if the portholes were not screwed tightly shut.

The *Florizel* thumped sluggishly along; sprindrift, flying over her deck, blended with the icy rain. Captain Martin, favoring the shelter of the starboard wing, stared out over the ugly sheen of steep whitecaps dancing off into the darkness.

Was she fully opened out below? he wondered. She must be, he decided once again; the chief engineer had not informed him otherwise. The sea and wind hitting her broadside *had* to be slowing her down. He could almost convince himself that she was doing a full seven knots, but he entered the chartroom and wrote in the logbook the speed of six knots. To be on the safe side he mentally gave her a speed of only five knots and jotted that down, too, in the margin of the logbook.

Allowing a speed of six knots since midnight, she should be off Cape Ballard, he estimated; on the sou'-sou'west course since midnight, she was in deep water, at least 10 miles off land. In fact, she was so far offshore that if she continued on the sou'-sou'west course too long, she would wind up too far out in the Atlantic and have to steam back north to get on course again. Unthinkable, when she was so many hours behind schedule.

South of Cape Ballard, the coast angled slightly westward, and the usual course of the *Florizel* from Cape Ballard was west-southwest. Studying his position on the chart, he decided to continue on the south-southwest course away from land until 4:00 A.M. Then he would haul her over for the approach to Cape Race. This course would take her past Cape Race about four miles offshore; by six o'clock they'd be around the cape and on the way to Halifax. She was five hours behind schedule, but she'd make up for lost time once she rounded Cape Race.

Captain Martin told King, "We'll haul her over at four o'clock."

Just as eight bells struck, Captain Martin gave the order, the wheel spun, and the bow of the *Florizel* swung from south-southwest to west-southwest.

# CHAPTER 7

*THE WATCHES* changed. First Officer James took over from Second Officer King, Gunner Hatchard was relieved by Gunner Curtis. Dooley, Gover, and Molloy replaced Green, Bailey, and Crocker.

In the engine room, Second Engineer Thomas Lumsden took over from Eric Collier and asked, "How is she going?"

Collier replied, "Everything all right," adding, "watch her a bit, she was racing."

He left, and Lumsden noted that the steam pressure was 170 pounds, but according to the blackboard, the number of revolutions she had averaged an hour was 63. The *Florizel* had really lost speed during the middle watch.

Ashes from the middle watch littered the deck of the stokehold and Lumsden ordered them ejected.

Although she was ejecting ashes, the *Florizel* picked up speed almost immediately on the west-southwest course. The wind and the sea were now on her port quarter pushing her along.

The seas grew wilder, rearing up in unrestrained fury; gusts of wind sheared off wavetops and hurled them on the deck. Heavy seas fell over the port quarter, spilled across the deck, and ran in under the port door of the social hall. The water saturated the carpet and dribbled over the ornate stairway to the deck below. Somewhere, a skylight shattered.

The *Florizel* complained noisily with loud thuds and crashes as every movable object rolled about the rooms and alleyways. Dishes shattered, cutlery jingled noisily, unusual rattles and creakings sounded throughout the ship.

Portholes were leaking everywhere. In Room 29, Captain Belleveau awakened to find his berth soaked and water sloshing around the floor. He leapt out of bed, closed the porthole tightly, dressed, then went in search of a steward to mop up the water. Noah Dauphinee, in the upper berth, slept soundly on.

Belleveau found Chief Steward Snow, who promptly went to look for a steward. Belleveau returned to his stateroom long enough to shake Dauphinee awake. "The room's awash, Noah," he said as Dauphinee opened his eyes. Then he left.

Chief Steward Snow was slightly harried. The stewards were all busy mopping up sea water in the staterooms aft, but he delegated Waiter Alex Fleet to clean up Belleveau's room. Noting the water dripping down over the stairway, he checked the social hall, saw that it, too, was awash, and passed orders to Charlie Reelis, another waiter, to get there quickly and start drying-up operations.

In Room 24, at the bottom of the stairway on the starboard side, William Parmiter had not gone to bed at all. It was not his first sea voyage, but it was the roughest; the creaking, banging, and fierce plunging of the ship were unsettling. Earlier, old Mr. Connolly had requested a drink of water and Parmiter had staggered to the washroom and fetched a carafe of fresh water. Now, alarmed at the ship's wild movements, he opened the door to take a look around and saw the sea trickling down the stairs and running along the floor. In great alarm he rushed through the passageways until he found the chief steward. "There's water coming down over the stairs!" he cried.

Snow replied, "That's the sea, Mr. Parmiter; it's coming in under the door of the social room." He added, "We're keeping it under control."

The chief steward seemed unconcerned, and Parmiter returned to his room to sit uneasily on the settee.

On the other side of the stairway, in Room 26, Minnie Denief was still too sick to be frightened by the wild tossing of the ship. Elizabeth Pelley had made no sound for hours; she was either asleep or dead, Minnie reasoned, though how anyone could sleep when the ship was tossing like a cork was beyond her.

The girls' stateroom was a mess: their suitcases slid around the floor; their clothing lay in scrambled heaps. Minnie's stomach and her whole world were upside down; she was wide awake in the middle of a nightmare.

The door opened and Charlie Snow stepped tentatively inside. "Is everything all right, Miss Denief?"

"I'm dying," Minnie groaned.

He joked, "Oh, come now, nobody ever dies on the *Florizel*." He added sympathetically, "It's a very bad night, Miss Denief."

He did not attempt to straighten the room. With a few encouraging words about its soon being over, he left.

The wind was backing to the east, gusting heavily, and the seas grew even steeper. In the social hall, the bookcase doors crashed open and books hurtled onto the floor. Major Sullivan, sleeping fitfully, came to full consciousness with a start. In the gloom of the hall, the piano rattled, hummed, and vibrated; the piano stool, held to the floor by one iron loop, had capsized and rolled in a noisy arc, crashing against the piano with each roll of the ship. The doors of the bookcase slammed open and shut with maddening regularity as the ship seesawed from port to starboard and back.

The major threw aside his blanket. There was, it seemed, to be no rest for him this night. Trying to maintain his balance, he staggered to the bookcase, cast around for something to jam it shut, found a pencil in his pocket, wedged it in the two brass loops on each door, and had the grim satisfaction of· stopping that noise. He returned to the sofa and sat uneasily. He noted that, while he had dozed, two other sofas had become occupied, and one of the occupants was a woman,* but who she was he could not tell. Doubtless, the two passengers, like himself, had found their staterooms too stuffy to tolerate.

He settled back onto the sofa, but with the wild tossing, the crashing stool, the singing piano, and the creaks and noises it was impossible to sleep. He was unaware of the constant inflow of water under the port door until three stewards rushed in with mops and pails, turned up the lights, and proceeded to mop up. For the first time Major Sullivan noticed that the hall was practically awash.

"Sorry, sir," Reelis said, "but we've got to clean up the water."

The major braced himself against the sofa. "It's certainly rough," he observed.

"We're having a time of it, sir; one of the skylights broke and one of the rooms† is flooded."

Sullivan did not really care about a stateroom being flooded; the thing that took priority right now was the

---

* Most likely, Mabel Barrett.
† Belleveau's room.

severe rolling and pitching of the ship and the loss of sleep. He needed sleep and the lack of it tonight did not put him in the most amiable mood, but, resigned to wakefulness, he gathered up his blanket, rose, and zigzagged aft. If John Munn was awake, he would visit for a spell.

Waiters Jimmy Dwyer and John Johnston were awakened by the violent motion of the ship and the seas leaking in through the porthole of the stewards' quarters on the starboard side of the ship. Dwyer got up, mopped up the water, then decided to stay up, since it was impossible to sleep in such a racket. He was not on duty until 5:00 A.M. but he might as well start work early. After the last few hectic hours (if he was any judge), there was going to be a major clean-up job on the *Florizel*.

He dressed, tidied their quarters as best he could, then putting on his coveralls, headed for the promenade deck to check on the needs of John Munn, their most important passenger. Johnston stayed in bed.

The *Florizel* was running freely before the wind and sea. Captain Martin was pleased with her speed now. If she had been laggard before, she was making up for lost time, bounding ahead, showing her heels to the snarling sea. In spite of the turbulence, she had not once put her head under.

The driving force of the rain had lessened slightly and visibility was up to a mile, maybe more, and he would not have been surprised to see the glimmering of the powerful Cape Race light at any moment. It had been a rough voyage after they had run out of the protection of the sish ice an hour back, but they would be around Cape Race by six o'clock at the latest, and from then on it would be plain sailing.

It was getting up to 4:30 A.M. when a deep rumble, like the sound of thunder, came from beneath the bridge; they felt the heavy vibrations in the soles of their feet. The ship lurched violently and someone shouted, "The cargo's adrift in number-two hold."

Martin bellowed, "Dooley, get the carpenter and the bos'un to secure the cargo!"

The rumbles grew louder with each pitch and roll of the ship, and Dooley went swiftly from the bridge to the forecastle where the carpenter, Jacob Pinsent, and the bos'un, Michael Power, had their quarters with the other seamen, including Joe Burry, George Crocker, Thomas Green, and John Lambert. The oilers and the Spanish firemen had their quarters there also, but tonight, only two firemen and one oiler, Edward Timmons, were there.

It was deafening in the forecastle, the din of the seas smashing under the flat bottom of the bow was like the explosions of big guns, but Dooley had to shake the men to awaken them. "Cargo's adrift in number-two hold; the Cap'n says you gotta fix it," he shouted.

The men tumbled out of their berths while Dooley swiftly returned to the bridge. Below, rolling casks of fish collided with other casks as they plunged from one side of the hold to the other. Tumbling, rolling, splintering, they would eventually batter other casks supporting the rest of the cargo, and that could be hellishly dangerous.

On the bridge, Martin listened uneasily to the runaway fish casks. If the cargo got out of hand and caused the *Florizel* to list, she might become unmanageable in the heavy seas. Very soon now he would change course to go around Cape Race, and that would ease the strain all round.

They had not gone through any more strings of ice for the past hour, and he ordered the log out. Mistaking the order, Dooley picked up the sounding tube, minus an inner glass tube, went aft with Gover, and cast. Mate James did not supervise the casting since the log had been ordered out, and the log did not require his supervision. The two sailors measured 90 fathoms before the lead struck bottom and Dooley reported back to the Captain, "Ninety fathoms of wire, sir."

Captain Martin regarded him with mild exasperation. "I didn't tell you to cast the lead, Dooley, I told you to put the log over." He added: "No matter, I'm casting at five o'clock unless I see Cape Race light, but put the log over *now*."

The two men hastened aft.

Martin consulted his chart. The lead had been cast without the chemically treated glass tube and without the supervision of the officer-in-charge, therefore, officially, the sounding could not be an absolutely reliable one. Nevertheless, with the ship bounding along at a good 10 knots, half the wire running out would correspond to the depth of water beneath her keel, and that meant they were in 45 fathoms of water. According to the chart, and his estimation of her position, this put the *Florizel* practically upon the northern end of the Ballard Banks, about 11 miles offshore and roughly six miles northward of Cape Race, which was where he expected to be. Now that he knew where he was, he decided it would be feasible to change course to go around Cape Race.

He told Mate James where they were and that they would alter course shortly.

At that moment the harried-looking chief steward appeared on the bridge. "Cap'n, the portholes are leaking, the passengers are complaining, and a sea came right in through Captain Belleveau's porthole. His room's awash."

Martin was unperturbed. "Never mind, Charlie; we'll

soon be altering to west by south. It'll be easier going, then."

Snow was relieved. Altering course would put the wind and the sea on the *Florizel's* stern and the portholes would stop leaking.

Major Sullivan tapped on the door of John Munn's room, and was told to come in. Munn was in his berth, clinging to the sideboard. His room was a mess. Bracing himself, he sat up, waved to the settee. "Sit down, Mike."

"I couldn't sleep with the ship rolling the way she is," Sullivan growled.

Munn put his feet against the settee. "I've never known the *Florizel* to roll like this, not ever. Put your feet against my berth; you'll be able to brace yourself better."

Sullivan did so just as the steward, Jimmy Dwyer, appeared at the door. "Can I get you gentlemen anything? Some fruit maybe?'

"Some fruit will be fine, Jimmy," Munn replied.

Before leaving, Dwyer tucked John Munn's luggage more securely under his berth. "I don't know how long it'll stay there, sir, but I'll be right back with some oranges," he said as he left.

At 4:40 A.M., judging the ship to be off Cape Race, Captain Martin ordered a change in course for her to go around. "Haul 'er over, west by south," he told the wheelsman, William Molloy.

Molloy hauled her over.

John Johnston had not slept after Dwyer left. It began to nag at him that a case of jams he had put in the storeroom might well be a mess of splintered glass by now. The passengers just might be without jam for breakfast in a few hours' time, and that would never do.

He thought about it for a little while longer; Dwyer had not returned and Johnston knew it was likely he had his hands full drying out the passengers' accommodations, and *he* had better make sure there would be jam for their breakfast.

He got up, dressed, and made his way forward to the storeroom.

John Munn and Michael Sullivan accepted an orange each from Dwyer. The suitcases were again tumbling about the room and this time he left them. Bracing themselves between berth and settee, Sullivan and Munn peeled and ate their oranges. There could be no thought of rest or sleep now; they could only hold on.

Sullivan rose, clinging to the top berth for support. "I think I'll go on deck and see what it's all about," he said.

"Do that; then come back and tell me what's going on, will you?"

"Right you are." Sullivan lurched toward the door just as Dwyer poked his head inside again. "Do you need anything else, Mr. Munn?" he asked.

Munn replied, "No, thank you."

Dwyer ducked out into the alleyway and Sullivan followed. From the social hall the voices of the stewards were raised above the din, their buckets clanking as the men mopped. Sullivan worked his way aft. He would take a look out through the door leading to the deck.

Jackman had slept fitfully until four o'clock when the ship's rough movements jostled him to full consciousness, and he had lain uneasily, ears attuning to the chaotic mutterings of the ship. Sleep would not return and he did not go on duty until eight o'clock, so he did what he had frequently done before: got one of his books from the drawer and began to study. He was soon to take exams for his ticket as a second officer, and he used any available free moments for study. This was as good a time as any.

Farther aft in the crews' quarters, Henry Dodd and his roommate, Cook Harry Lynch had both been awakened when they were nearly flung from their berths. "Oh well," Henry said, philosophically, "it's nearly time to get up anyway."

"Ah," Harry agreed, yawning, "we might as well get up."

They dressed and made their way to the kitchen for an early breakfast. The ship was laboring mightily, strange creaks and groans assailed their ears from all sides as they lurched along the passageway. Even as they approached the kitchen they could hear the clatter of cutlery and dishes, the discord of pots and pans banging hollowly together. They would have one hell of a time getting breakfast while this sea was on.

# CHAPTER 8

*ON THE* bridge, Captain Martin peered through the black night. He was confident that as soon as they rounded Cape Race and ran under the lee of the land, the sea would lose much of its fury. They were, he estimated, in the process of rounding the Cape, and passengers would shortly be able to rest easier; the cargo would be secured.

Beside him, First Officer James peered through the night and thought he saw something solid white ahead.

*Ice!*

Was that more ice glimmering on the black sea?

A sleety rain still raked the ship, but he could see up to three-quarters of a mile, he estimated.

*Was* that ice ahead?

His eyes narrowed. It looked like one of the strings they had been passing through earlier; he could see the dark sea beyond.

Captain Martin saw it at the same time. "What's that?" he snapped. "It looks like ice."

"Yes, it does," James agreed, but to be sure he examined the white line through the binoculars as they pitched and rolled toward it. He said slowly, "Yes, I believe it is."

Martin also scrutinized it through the binoculars as the *Florizel* hurtled onward. It *was* ice, he decided. "Probably a string of slob coming around the Cape."

Between them, they decided to their satisfaction, it was just that, and Mate James told Dooley: "Better get aft and haul in the log, or we'll lose it going through the ice."

Dooley and Gover went aft to haul in the log.

The *Florizel*, steaming a good nine to 10 knots, with the wind and sea snarling on her port quarter, bounded along toward the white line.

*But the white line was not a string of ice, it was a white line of breakers 250 yards offshore from Horn Head Point, Cappahayden, 45 miles along the coast from Cape Spear, 12 miles north of Cape Race.*

There was a grinding, screeching crash of metal on rock as the *Florizel* piled onto the reef. Riding high on the crest of a swell, she fell on the rocks, hitting under number-two hold, to be lifted by a following wave and carried farther over the rocks. A third time she was lifted and dropped in a welter of furious seas. Her foretopmast crashed to the foredeck, rocks gouged and tore her hull; then, securely impaled, she began to grind and settle to the starboard. Cradled on a slope with bow up and stern down, the proud *Florizel* was mortally wounded, with a gaping hole in her starboard side and the bottom torn out of her.

Captain Martin had run her full speed upon Horn Head Reef.

Above the pandemonium Mate James shouted unbelievingly, "She's ashore."

Martin had already jammed the telegraph to "Full Astern" and the *Florizel*, jumping and bouncing around, sent passengers and crew spinning; there was a scream of tearing metal as she cracked just aft of the smoke-stack.

White-faced, Martin gave the order to James: "Get the lifeboats cleared away and ready." To another sailor, he barked, "Tell the operator to get out an S.O.S." Chief Steward Snow had appeared on the bridge and Martin rasped, "Get all passengers on deck and get out the lifebelts." To the crew on the bridge, he yelled, "Everybody get their lifebelts."

Those orders given, he turned on the automatic whistle to alert everybody aboard to the fact that the ship was in distress. There was no time to think about where she was or why she had run ashore, although he was sure in his heart and soul it was very near Cape Race.

Then, because she was an obstruction to its forward drive, the ocean gathered in upon itself and lifted over her port quarter to smash upon her deck. Great combers surged up over her port side, heaved over the bulwarks to explode against the superstructure with awesome force. Ladders and doors on the port side gave way and the sea rushed in through the social hall, cascaded down over the great ornate stairway, and fell through the circular opening above the dining saloon.

Skylights were shattered. The seas swept her diagonally on the promenade deck; the port doorway aft leading into the first-class section, and the starboard doorway leading to the officers' quarters below, shook ominously. The crash had shifted many of the wartime blackouts on the superstructure and, like a leviathan, she lay there, her lights blazing, her automatic whistle wailing as the heavy seas toyed with her.

PART III

# Shipwreck

CHAPTER 9

*THERE WAS* uncertainty in the first moments of the wreck. An astonishing number thought she had entered a heavy icefield; the clanging and jolting was not unlike a ship steaming through heavy ice. But with the grinding noises, the blasts of her automatic whistle, and the slope and list of the ship, there was a gradual increase of pandemonium as passengers began their fight for survival, fleeing their staterooms to make for the upper regions of the ship.

It had been a quiet watch for John Bernard Murphy in the Marconi room. When the ship struck, it did not occur to him in the first moments that it was disaster. But he was jarred and tumbled from one side of the tiny room to the other most alarmingly, and when her gyrations began to subside slightly, the continual blasting of the ship's whistle, the shouting outside, sent him staggering to the door. He poked his head outside and was able to discern other men tumbling about the boat deck. Even as it dawned on him that the ship was in difficulties, a sailor rushed out of the night, bellowing, "Cap'n said to send an S.O.S.!"

Murphy, as he had been drilled to do many times by

Carter, sent an S.O.S. three times on the private wire rigged to Room 21. He was not permitted to send out calls himself, but he proceeded to get the emergency apparatus in readiness in the event it would be needed. To get the generator working properly, it had to be cranked slowly.

In a few minutes Carter burst into the room, haphazardly dressed, with his clothes unbuttoned and his shoes untied. In his arms he carried a couple of blankets that he had grabbed from his berth. "Where are we?" he gasped.

Murphy had just turned over the starting handle of the generator. "I don't know," he yelled. The *Florizel* was still rolling on the rocks and he had difficulty keeping his balance.

Carter bawled, "Then phone the bridge and get our position from the Captain!"

Flinging himself at the key, he began transmitting while Murphy tried to phone through to the bridge. There was no reply. "I can't get any answer on the phone," he roared. "I'll have to go to the bridge."

Carter was already tapping out: "*S.O.S. S.O.S. S.O.S. Florizel.*"

Engineer John Lumsden knew it was not ice that she had hit. The force with which she had struck was unmistakable. The concussion of ship on rock numbed all senses. The Spanish firemen who had been sleeping in the stokehold were thrown to the floor. The three firemen, the coal-passer, Oiler John Davis, and Lumsden pitched from one side of the engine room to the other.

The bouncing and rolling subsided slightly when she listed to starboard, her powerful engine still throbbing. Lumsden immediately ran to the reverse gear, anticipating the orders from the bridge to go full astern. As the engine strained to back her off the reef, there was a sound of screaming metal and rushing water; the *Florizel* had cracked in the middle and the ocean was rushing in on the starboard side.

Davis yelled, "Come on, let's get out of here!"

Lumsden was like a man of stone. He did not answer Davis, but waited at the telegraph for orders from the bridge, whatever they might be. Davis waited for a couple of precious minutes, then, receiving no further orders, fled to warn the other engineers. The firemen, wearing only singlets and pants, followed Davis but rushed forward through the dining saloon, up the stairs to the social hall, and on up to the boat deck, stationing themselves by one of the lifeboats.

No orders came to Lumsden from the bridge. The ship continued to grind on the rocks, shuddering and screeching as her engine labored to haul her off the reef, and he waited for an interminable five or six minutes as the sea poured into the engine room and crept up around his legs. He knew with sickening finality there was nothing more he could do, nothing anyone could do. He turned the engine off, waded through sea water already surging up around his knees, and climbed the iron stairs to the dynamo, opening the steam on it. As long as the steam in the boilers lasted, it would feed the dynamo and keep the lights, whistle, and wireless apparatus operating until the sea flooded the engine room.

The engine cranks were still working when Lumsden took one last heartsick look at the sea rushing around the engine before he left.

As the *Florizel* crashed upon the reef, Philip Jackman hurtled across his cabin. The tearing sound of metal gave him no illusions about ice. He grabbed his trousers, dressing as swiftly as the gyrations of the ship permitted, and when she settled, John McKinnon, the baker, and Arthur Moody, the butcher, poked anxious faces into his room. "Is it ice, Mr. Jackman?" McKinnon asked.

Grabbing his overcoat, Jackman said, "No, boys, it's rocks she got now." They appeared to be rooted to the deck, and he yelled, "Look out for yourselves!" Then he left on the run for the bridge.

In the stern, Dooley and Gover had been about to haul in the log when they were thrown to the deck. "She's on the rocks," Dooley yelled.

They scrambled to their feet, zigzagged to the ladders that took them up to the boat deck, and reeled forward to the bridge.

Bos'un Michael Power, Jacob Pinsent, the carpenter, and seamen Burry, Crocker, Lambert, and Green were still in the forecastle making ready to tackle the runaway cargo. They tumbled about the narrow confines of their quarters; Edward Timmons and the Spanish firemen were thrown from their berths.

Their shouts of alarm were lost in the frightful uproar, and when the *Florizel* subsided and listed to starboard, Pinsent and Power leapt to the foredeck to sprint for the bridge. Green was immediately behind them. Burry, Crocker, Lambert, Timmons, and the two Spaniards were still in the shelter of the forecastle when the first sea lifted over the port side, thundered across the deck and smashed into the bulkhead. It swept Pinsent, Power, and Green to the starboard rail where they hung on as the wave went over them. When it had passed, they made a dash for the ladder that took them up to the boat deck.

Burry and Lambert found themselves hanging onto the door of the lamp room on the port side of the forecastle; as the sea pulled back they tumbled inside and shut the door. They were soaked and chilled, but safe. The two Spanish firemen had disappeared. Oiler Timmons had made it to the protection of the superstructure and was making his way aft.

Burry, collecting his wits, immediately thought of Crocker. He opened the door to see if there was any sign of him, and saw him hanging on to a stanchion.

"In here, George," he bawled.

Crocker heard, gave a dissenting wave of the hand, and made a dash for the superstructure.

Then the seas were raking the ship.

Pinsent, Power, and Green arrived on the boat deck in time to hear the captain pass out orders to get the lifeboats cleared away. Dooley, Gover, and Philip Jackman dashed on the scene about the same time. Crocker made it moments later.

They all dispersed to the lifeboats — three on the port side, three on the starboard.

Major Michael Sullivan had been halfway along the alleyway to the port door, aft, when the *Florizel* struck. He was thrown backward, then flung side to side as she slammed over the rocks. The whistle began to blast, and immediately, frightened passengers burst out of their staterooms. Then the seas hit the *Florizel* with a deep, ringing explosion such as they had never heard before, and terror struck them to the heart as the ship shuddered violently.

Stewards Dwyer and Snow were in the main alleyway. Charlie Reelis, Stanley Foley, and Austin Whitten were still in the social hall, though they had been scattered and pitched in every direction. Then Chief Steward Snow came on the run from the bridge, shouting orders: "All passengers get dressed and take their lifebelts!"

Over the clamor of the ship and the boom of exploding seas, the stewards bellowed, "All hands out, the ship's ashore! All hands out!"

It broke the spell that had gripped many passengers. Now there were cries of fear as they suddenly came to life, milling around the narrow alleyway. Major Sullivan made his way through them to John Munn's room, poked his head inside. John Munn was standing, barefoot, pants in one hand.

"She's on the rocks, John!" he shouted.

Above the deep blasting of the ship's whistle, Munn asked, "Is it bad?"

"I don't know," Sullivan yelled.

Munn tossed aside his pants, put on his gray overcoat, and stepped out into the melee of shouting passengers. Sullivan saw his friend slide and slip down the canting deck toward Room 18, where his little daughter Betty and her nurse, Evelyn Trenchard, slept.

Suddenly the port door of the social hall burst in and a torrent of water flooded across the hall and tumbled in a cataract down the stairway. Following seas surged through the door and swept along the alleyway toward him. Sullivan came to life, hopping quickly into his own room.

John P. Kieley was still in the smoker when the ship struck. At the moment of impact, only two other passengers were with him, Captain Joe Kean and one whose identity* was never made known. Still somewhat inebriated, Kieley had been taking his companions into the fascinating world of moving pictures.

Conversation ceased and Captain Kean muttered, "We've hit the ice."

From forward, over the horrendous noise of the ship, came cries and shouts of alarm and the steady blasting

* Most likely Captain Belleveau.

of the whistle. Joe Kean reached for his overcoat. "I'm going to see what's wrong," he said.

The other man grabbed his coat. "I'll go with you."

"So will I," Kieley murmured. Drunk as he was, his brain was functioning clearly.

The two men left. Kieley did not have his overcoat, and when he followed them outside, the stinging cold pierced his clothing. He changed his mind about going forward. He had better get his overcoat first, he thought, and went through the door leading to the first-class section below.

Nobody was around, it seemed, as he carefully maneuvered the stairs, retaining his equilibrium in spite of the awkward angle and the rolling hull. Suddenly, at the foot of the stairs, people were milling and shouting in excitement. "What happened?" he was asked. "Is it ice?" They did not seem to expect a reply and went on asking each other the same questions, so Kieley, murmuring words of comfort, passed serenely through them.

He recognized the plump, comfortable form of the stewardess, Margaret Keough, and found that she was with him as he negotiated the alleyway to his stateroom. Whether she was helping him or he was helping her was a moot point; she was beside him — that was all he was aware of.

As a soldier, Major Sullivan was used to emergency measures. The deafening noise of seas exploding on the walls of his stateroom told him that the port side of the ship was taking the brunt of the sea, and he knew the lights would not last long, not the way the sea was inundating the *Florizel*.

He coolly opened his small suitcase, took out a flashlight, put on his greatcoat and cap, and stepped back into the alleyway. The water was surging in through the social hall, effectively blocking escape that way, and the alleyway aft was filled with milling people, so he went through the cross-alleyway (outside Room 19) to the starboard side and hurried aft, and therefore did not meet John Kieley, who was making his way through the crowd to their room. Nor did Sullivan see John Munn.

Only a small group of people had so far gathered on the stairway leading to the boat deck, but more were coming from behind as Sullivan made his way, unimpeded, up the stairs. At the top he saw some of his companions of a few hours back standing dazed and in shock. Smythe was there in his pajamas, William Wright was wearing pants only, C. H. Miller (carrying suitcases) and Tom McNeil were both fully dressed. Someone shouted that they would need warm clothing, and several people rushed back down the stairs.

Sullivan decided to go forward and offer assistance to the captain and crew. He stepped outside on the boat deck and, propelled by the wind, slid to the starboard. Grabbing the handrailing, he hauled himself around to the lee of the smoker and, with the aid of his flashlight, found it surprisingly easy to pick his way along the deck. He had reached the smokestack when he heard Joe Kean's voice above the uproar of ship and sea. He was shouting, "Let's see if we can get a boat out."

Kean was with a group of men struggling to cut the canvas from one of the lifeboats on the port deck.

"Nothing can live in that sea," a voice roared back.

Sullivan was conscious of other forms struggling with other lifeboats. He was aware of all of these things as he hugged the shelter of the smokestack.

Waiter Henry Dodd and Cook Harry Lynch were in the kitchen attempting to prepare an early breakfast when the ship struck. Dishes broke and pots and pans clattered from the pantry to the kitchen to dance and roll on the floor with the two men as they were pitched around.

Henry gave a surprised shout. "That's some heavy ice!"

No thought of shipwreck entered their minds; they did not equate the proud *Florizel* with disaster. But as she ground on over the rocks, it was apparent that something out of the ordinary was happening. When she listed to the starboard and her whistle began to blast, Henry collected his scattered wits. "We'd better take a look outside," he yelled.

Crawling through cutlery and broken crockery, they reached the kitchen door on the starboard side and slid into the alleyway in time to see Chief Engineer Reader come from his own room and head for the quarters of the engineers. "Collier! Taylor!" he was shouting.

Dodd did not realize how bad the disaster was until he took a hasty look down into the engine room. For one paralyzed moment he stared at the seas swirling around the engine, then he turned and fled. He moved swiftly along the alleyway, then darted through the cross-alleyway, which sloped upward because of the list but at this moment presented no obstacle. Reaching the port alleyway, he ducked around the corner and up the stairs to the first-class deck.

As yet there had been no time for passengers to realize fully what had happened; they were half in and half out of their staterooms, asking each other what was wrong. Suddenly Dodd remembered his old employer, W. F. Butler, and made for Room 15 in the starboard alleyway. He pounded on the door, shouting, "Get up, Mr. Butler, the ship's on the rocks. Get up, sir!"

Butler opened the door. He looked pale and frightened, but he was partially dressed, with his overcoat on over his pajamas. Mrs. Butler was reaching for her fur coat, which she put on over her nightdress. Neither she nor her husband nor Dodd thought of lifebelts. "We'd better get to the boat deck, sir; she's filling with water," Dodd shouted.

Butler picked up the small black bag that he had carried earlier and passed it to Henry. It was quite heavy. "Hold on to it for me, Henry," he said.

"Right, sir," Dodd replied, and carrying the black bag he led the way aft, holding Mrs. Butler by the hand. Butler took her other hand. They reached the stairway and ascended quickly in spite of the awkward angle of the stairs.

William Butler opened the door and slipped out on the deck; his wife and Dodd followed. The after-end of the ship was gradually disappearing, and a comber surged up over the boat deck, sweeping the three of them to the starboard rail. Henry involuntarily let go of Mrs. Butler and the little black bag* in order to save himself from being swept overboard. He found himself clinging to the sea rail staring at the furious surf beneath his feet. He made a lunge for the handrailing around the smoker, grabbed it, and huddled in its shelter.

In the passageway, the stewards raced through the ship, shouting at the top of their lungs, "All hands on deck, the ship's ashore!"

Only Dwyer went to each stateroom in his section to warn the passengers to take their lifebelts; then, having done his duty, he thought of himself and dashed below to get a coat to protect himself against the weather. Still shouting a warning to all and sundry, he raced down over the stairs to the second-class section, slid down the cross-alleyway into the crew's quarters. "All hands out, the ship's ashore!" he bawled.

John Johnston had been on his way to the storeroom to check on the carton of jams when the *Florizel* struck.

* Relatives revealed to the author that Mr. Butler carried 10,000 dollars in the black bag.

Steward Stanley Squires was in the alleyway, and both men were flung from one side to the other. Squires cried, "She's in some heavy ice."

Johnston agreed and continued on to the storeroom, bouncing off the walls as he went, but the unusual motions of the ship and the blaring whistle made him forget the jams. He got out of the storeroom quickly. Squires had disappeared but he nearly collided with Dwyer who raced into the alleyway.

"We'd better get our lifebelts and overcoats," Johnston said.

They dashed to their quarters at a lurching half-run, grabbed their overcoats and lifebelts, struggling into them as they raced to the stairs that led to the first-class section on the promenade deck.

Fred Roberts, third cook, had actually slept before the ship piled on the reef. He awakened at the moment of impact and realized that he had heard it all before! The grinding, clanking, screeching noises were the same piercing nightmare sounds in his dream of yesterday.

He leapt out of bed, grabbed his pants, and somehow got into them. As the ship listed to starboard, he fled his quarters in bare feet, wearing only his singlet on top. All around, the horrendous noise of the stricken ship beat with frightening familiarity on his consciousness. Almost blind with fear, he navigated the sloping alleyway into the passenger section, where he collided with passenger Leonard Nicholls.

Nicholls turned a white face to him. "Is it serious?" he asked.

Roberts, recalling his dream, said grimly, "I think it's all up with us."

With Nicholls behind him he staggered on to the stairway that would take them to the first-class deck, and from there, to the boat deck.

Dave Griffiths and William Dodd awakened as the ship struck. Dave clung to his berth, but Dodd leapt to the floor, shouting, "Get up! Get up!"

Dave had traveled through ice in a steel ship once before, and the noise and commotion were almost identical. He shouted back, "What for? It's only the ice. She's in the ice."

William said fiercely, "Man, if you don't get up and dress, you'll die down here."

He was hanging on to the top berth, wearing only his long underwear. Letting go, he lurched out through the door. "You'd better hurry," he yelled, and was gone in a flash.

Dave braced himself in the berth trying to pull on his pants, but found himself on the floor. The ship fell to the starboard and the sound of the whistle urged him to hurry, but he dressed deliberately. If she was on the rocks, she was on the rocks, and if he was going to die, it was just as well for him to die down here as it was for him to die on deck, he thought. Indifferent health had long given him a stoical outlook on life, and death did not seem that terrifying.

As he dressed, he could not help reflecting on the strange ways of fate. When war had been declared, Dave had volunteered with the rest of his friends, but a weakness in his chest made him physically unfit. The doctor had declared, "You're a dead man if you ever let yourself get wet." Well, he thought, maybe I *am* a dead man.

He dressed fully except for one sock, which he could not find, then put on his overcoat and hat and left the room. He was unfamiliar with the ship, but a few people were about in the alleyway, all making for the stairway aft that lead to the first-class deck. Dave followed them.

In the stateroom next to Dave Griffiths, passengers Albert Fagan and R. F. Fowlow were still in their berths. They had been awake for hours, discussing the unusual roughness of the sea, and had made note of the position of the lifebelts (just in case); yet when she actually struck, both were sure it was only ice.

They heard someone outside shouting that she was ashore. "Did you hear that?" Fagan asked, more for confirmation that his ears were not deceiving him than anything else.

But Fowlow had often heard excited travelers hallucinating before. He said, "Naw, boy, she's just going through heavy ice."

They settled back, clinging to the sideboards as the ship continued to toss them around.

Along the alleyway toward the stern, John Cleary had lain in his berth, awake and uneasy. Paddy Fitzpatrick had slept soundly in the lower berth. When she hit, Cleary had to grab the sideboard to keep from being thrown to the floor. Paddy, jolted awake, cried out, "What is it? Is it the ice?"

Cleary jumped out of his berth. He had worked at sea all his life and knew disaster when it struck. "That's no ice, Paddy; let's get out of here!" he yelled.

He had slept in his underwear and undershirt; now he found his pants, hopped into them, shoved his bare feet into his shoes, then was out in the alleyway, staggering aft with Paddy on his heels. A passenger was struggling with two suitcases, blocking the way, and Cleary brushed past him. So did Paddy.

They floundered up over the companionway in the stern of the ship. Cleary pushed the door open and rushed on deck. With Paddy behind him, he dashed for the ladder leading to the boat deck. In less than a minute he and Paddy had reached the bridge and not a drop of water had touched them.

Gregory Maloney and James Crockwell were awakened from a sound sleep, but did not realize at first what had happened. Then the whistle began to blast, and the seas boiling around her stern hit the hull with frightening explosions of sound that made them sit bolt upright. "We better get dressed," Crockwell said.

Amidships, Captain James Bartlett and Joseph Stockley had awakened only when she struck. They concluded that she had steamed into heavy ice, and settled back in their berths.

In Room 29, forward of the dining saloon, Alex Fleet was mopping up sea water and Noah Dauphinee was watching from his berth. In spite of the fierce pitching and rolling of the ship, he would have returned to sleep as soon as Fleet left. When the *Florizel* struck, Fleet fell over backward and the bucket overturned, spilling its contents on the floor. Dauphinee was considerably shaken. "Is it ice?" he asked as she listed to starboard.

Fleet left the room without replying. The whistle began its steady blasting and Belleveau rushed into the room, "Get out, Noah, we're on the rocks," he bellowed, and just as abruptly left again.

With a seaman's agility, Dauphinee dressed fully with the exception of his shoes. He raced along the short alleyway to the ornate stairway leading to the social hall. Already this stairway was a waterfall of icy sea, but he mounted it three steps at a time. In the hall the water was rushing in through the port door. It creamed against sofas and tables on the starboard wall, funneling out through the starboard door; it surged around the shattered bookcase, rushed along the starboard wall, and flowed into the sloping alleyway aft. It fell like a Niagara down through the circular opening in the center of the hall.

Quickly, Dauphinee took all this in , then ran for the port alleyway. Reaching the stairway just as passengers were beginning to collect there, he did not pause but scrambled up the steps, got out on deck, and dashed into the smoker. It was crowded with frightened first-class passengers, and the whistle added to the nightmare. The skylight had shattered and it was bitterly cold.

With the impact, Minnie Denief sat bolt upright, seasickness forgotten. She was thrown violently about the berth, crying out in terror as the ship ground over the rocks. The *Florizel* itself seemed to be shrieking in terror.

Elizabeth Pelley sat up quickly. "What is it? What's wrong?" she asked.

The grinding ship told its own tale, and Elizabeth slipped from the top berth, casting about for her clothes. "Get up!" she ordered Minnie.

Minnie quavered, "I'm scared."

Elizabeth was the cool one. "Nothing to be scared about, but you'd better dress."

Minnie was groping frantically under her pillow. "Where are my glasses? I can't see without them," she cried.

Miraculously, she found them and put them on. She had only partially undressed and she scrabbled around trying to find something to put on. Her clothes were in a heap on the floor, and she picked up all the wrong things first, but eventually she found a thin little sweater and put it on.

Elizabeth was putting on her boots.

Archibald Gardiner, in Room 16 in the starboard alleyway, had not slept at all; he had been seasick all night and was utterly wretched. George Parmiter had come in late, incredibly falling into a sound sleep.

When the *Florizel* hit, Gardiner thought she had entered an icefield, but she clanged and rolled with such frightening force that he got out of bed to peer out of the small square window. Seeing nothing, he lurched back to his berth and climbed in. Parmiter had not moved through all the clamor.

Now the whistle began to blow and a voice was shouting outside his room. Gardiner rose again, this time poking his head out the door. He saw a steward running along the alleyway and knew that it was not ice the *Florizel* had hit. Seasickness forgotten, he shook Parmiter awake. "Wake up! Wake up! We're on the rocks," he shouted.

Parmiter tumbled out of bed and both men dressed hurriedly. Parmiter was first into the alleyway, pushing his way through the other passengers to reach the social hall. Gardiner trailed behind. He saw Parmiter reach the port door of the social hall just as a sea burst through. It flooded through the door in a solid wall of tumbling ocean, and Parmiter disappeared before his eyes. Gardiner retreated hastily.

The *Florizel* was swinging to and fro as the seas smashed against and over her with deep, shattering explosions. Gardiner made his way through the crowd, which was also heading aft in a confused sort of way. He stumbled up the stairs, stepped out on the boat deck, and ducked into the smoker. Many passengers were there, white and scared, and like himself, not dressed for the biting cold. Gardiner wasted no time. If this was a sample of what they were in for, he had better dress for it. He slipped out of the smoker, back inside the companionway, and made it through the crowd without difficulty. The port door aft was splitting under the battering seas, but it still held.

In his room, Gardiner put on his overcoat, took the time to remove some cash and his wristwatch from his suitcase, then stepped back into the alleyway. There was more water now, and it dragged him along as it rushed aft; in the cross-alleyway it was tumbling over the stairs to the second-class accommodations below. He made it to the stairway to find it blocked with people and luggage.

Alex Ledingham had leapt out of bed immediately the ship had struck. Robert Wright, in the lower berth, said, "She's in the heavy ice, I guess."

"That's not ice; you had better get your clothes on," Ledingham said grimly.

He hauled out his trunk, opened it, removed a suit of heavy green woollen underwear, and put it on. Ledingham had no illusions about the kind of night it was outside; he intended to be fully prepared.

Wright was dressing when Ledingham left the room. It was his intention to make for the bridge to help Captain Martin, but aft there was fright and confusion as passengers jammed the stairway. Over the noise a voice was shouting, "All passengers take their lifebelts!"

In the melee, Ledingham was shoved into any empty stateroom. He knew that every room carried a supply of lifebelts in the bottom drawer of the wardrobe and, checking it, found up to a dozen. He passed them out, keeping the last one for himself.

When the whistle continued to sound. Kitty Cantwell sat up. "What's going on?" she called out.

There was a pounding on her door, and Steward Snow shouted, "All hands on deck, the ship's ashore. All hands on deck!"

Kitty scrambled from her berth. "Did you hear that, Annie? We have to get dressed and get out of here."

She was already fumbling for her clothes which were strewn about the floor with everything else. "Get up, Annie! *Get up!*" she screamed.

Annie lay inert. Outside there was chaos, but she appeared to be oblivious of it all.

Kitty dressed swiftly, putting on her high stylish boots, her skirt and coat. She buttoned her boots right to the top, all the time urging Annie to get a move on. "Come on, Annie, we've got to get on deck!" she cried. "Hurry up, Annie, hurry up!"

When Annie still made no move to get up, Kitty grimly approached the berth to help her.

Stockley and Bartlett were used to the jolting of a ship going through ice, but they decided to have a look outside their stateroom to see what all the fuss was about. Stockley poked his head outside. The sea was rushing along the alleyway and for a moment he stared unbelievingly, then he gave a yell. "The bottom is out of 'er, Cap. We're sinking!"

Being seamen, they did not rush blindly out into the night, but quickly dressed, Stockley even putting on his cap and muffler. He had 150 dollars tucked away in his suitcase; it represented long months of saving, but there was no time to get it; the water was already flowing into their room. Life was sweeter than 150 dollars.

"Ready?" Bartlett yelled.

"Ready!" Stockley yelled back.

The sea was already up to their knees and rose swiftly to their thighs as they groped their way toward the sinking stern. They were unutterably relieved when they reached the companionway that led to the deck aft of the cargo winches behind number-three hold. All around them was the roar of rushing water; the stairway was a veritable river in flood.

They struggled upward.

Old Mr. Connolly was dozing when the *Florizel* struck. Sitting on the settee opposite the door, William Parmiter was thrown across the room as the ship ground over the reef. Above the other terrifying sounds, he became conscious of someone outside shouting, "All passengers out! All passengers out!"

Parmiter, greatly alarmed, opened the door and as he did so, water cascaded over the stairs, struck the door like a ton of bricks, and knocked him back into the room, pinning him to the settee. It flooded the room, surged around him. Parmiter finally thrashed his way to the cabin next door. He burst into the room to find John Connolly half dressed, lacing up his boots.

Agitated, Connolly asked, "Is Father up?"

Before Parmiter could reply, a second sea swept down over the stairs and he found himself floating around the passageway outside and carried along to the end of it. In fright and shock he floundered around, trying to regain his footing. There was no doubt in his mind that old Mr. Connolly was already drowned, and he would drown, too, if he did not get out of there fast.

He groped toward the stairs. Another torrent poured over him as he grasped the rail post. Catching his breath, he dragged himself upward to the social hall.

On the port side of the stairway, Minnie Denief heard the roar of water flooding down over the stairs, and sheer terror forced her to open the door. *She must not be trapped!*

The ship lurched violently to and fro, and without knowing how she got there, Minnie found herself out of her room, waist deep in the icy seas that thundered like a waterfall from the deck above. The piano, followed by other furniture, tumbled over the stairs, vibrating discordantly, and floated beside her. The rolling ship flung her, screaming in terror, against the walls, and through the double doors into the dining saloon. The piano followed. Before her horrified eyes a cataract of white water roared through the circular opening above.

*The* Florizel *was sinking! She had to get out of there!*

With fierce determination she began to fight her way back to the stairway when a sea hurled her against the wall of the saloon. Her glasses flew from her eyes and she went under.

Maloney and Crockwell dressed quickly, but the water was rushing through the steerage and flooding into their room by the time they were ready. As they paused in the main alleyway to get their bearings, young Billy Guzzwell appeared beside them. The boy was alone and he was crying. They continued aft, taking him with them.

Waves were piling in from the Atlantic, rearing to great heights and rolling shoreward in a seething, tumbling mass. They fell upon the *Florizel* with such violence as to preclude any attempt to rig lifelines. All such lines and safety equipment were swept away.

She shook continually, her metal plates clanking against the rocks. With the bottom torn out of her, the holds and the engine room filled quickly. The water, rushing through the narrow passageways on the lower deck, rose with deadly swiftness. Heavy swells billowed up over the port quarter to fall over on her deck and smash against the superstructure; they raked her diagonally, with the whole port side taking the brunt of the terrible force of the ocean.

Suddenly the port door aft burst inward, and the water tunneled in through the alleyway, boiling furiously as it smashed head on into the sea flowing back from the social hall. It rushed into the cross-alleyway at the foot of the smoker stairway, spilled over the stairs to the saloon deck. The same wave split the rear starboard door leading directly to the crew's quarters below. In a few minutes the cross-alleyway leading to the crew's quarters was a rushing torrent of water.

As the ocean invaded her, the wind carried her death cries in over the land.

CHAPTER **10**

*THE DEEP-TONED* voice of the ship's whistle brought the people of Cappahayden tumbling from their beds to stare in disbelief at the blazing lights of the great ship practically on their doorstep. *"Jaysus!* She's on Horn Head!"

The pounding seas boomed on the great beach sweeping in a rough semicircle from Horn Head to Burnt Head, with Cappahayden nestling close to Burnt Head. The wind whipped over the steep hills above the beach and whined around their homes, rattling windows and doors; sleet hit the windowpanes, and through it all glimmered the lights of the *Florizel*.

"She's done, that one is," muttered one fisherman.

"God help 'em," another said.

They knew that, when the southeast gales blew, the ocean rolled upon their shore with the force of a tidal wave, and Horn Head would be a mad, chaotic mass of tumbling seas, awesome in its destructive fury.

Quickly the men of Cappahayden dressed, put on oilskins, gathered ropes, lines, gaffs, any kind of gear that might come in handy, then made their way along the beach to Horn Head, about a mile away. The whole strand was a seething cauldron of white water cascading on the beach in a continuous barrage of explosions that made speech impossible.

There was little hope that anything could be done for those on the wrecked liner until the seas died down.

# CHAPTER 11

DEVASTATED BY hours of illness, Annie Dalton did not seem to realize the seriousness of the situation. Having been tossed about the berth for hours, she was now seemingly unmindful of the violent convulsions of the ship. Kitty shook her friend, screaming, "We're on the rocks, Annie, we've got to get out of here."

Annie sat up and, with Kitty's help, eased groggily out of the top berth, but collapsed weakly on the lower berth. "I can't," she moaned.

In desperation, Kitty knelt, forced the boots on Annie's feet, and buttoned them haphazardly. "They're not done up very tight, Annie, but they'll do." She was panting with exertion and fright. "Now get up and we'll put your coat on!"

Wearing only her underclothes, Annie stood while Kitty forced her arms into her coat. The alarming sound of rushing water, the banging, shouting, and confusion, were horribly frightening, and Kitty had no idea what to expect outside their room.

"We'd better get out of here," she said.

Without thinking of the lifebelts that Steward Ivany had shown them earlier, she opened the door and stepped into the passageway, dragging Annie with her. Both shrieked as they found themselves knee deep in the icy water rushing along the passage. Kitty had a confused picture of men and women struggling against the sea and of a girl with dark hair who fell in through the open door of their stateroom.

In the crew's quarters, Alex Fleet was pounding the door of the room he shared with Gordon Ivany. It was locked and his own key was inside; Ivany, apparently, had locked it when he left.

Fleet did not give up easily; he needed his overcoat and was determined to get it if he had to beat the door down, and that is what he intended to do. The nearest emergency axe was in the cross-alleyway on the deck above, and Fleet, knowing every inch of the ship, was up and back with an axe in less than a minute. Disregarding the water flooding the alleyway, he attacked the door but the solid mahogany barely dented under the puny blows of the axe. After a few more minutes Fleet threw the axe aside and fled for his life.

Cook Joseph Moore was still in his room when the sea split the door leading to the crew's quarters. He had not been asleep when the *Florizel* struck, and had waited until the ship's convulsions died before attempting to dress. It was a wild night and he had no intention of rushing headlong outside half clothed.

He dressed fully, taking the valuables he had in his locker, and the lower deck was in flood by the time he was ready. The incline leading to the passengers' section was a swift-flowing stream, but he hauled himself up by the handrailing, ducked through the waterfall pouring over the stairs, and joined the passengers clustered in the smoker stairway.

The sea was spilling into the engine room when Lumsden emerged from below. He was jostled roughly as water tumbled through the wrecked companionway; soon, she would be completely inundated. He wasted no time. He had 700 dollars and valuable papers locked away in his room.

Suddenly, floundering toward him was Herbert Taylor. White-faced and with eyes staring, he shouted, "The Chief called me. What happened?"

Lumsden shouted back, "It's no use going below; better get topside."

He continued on toward his room to salvage his papers and money. The valuables were locked in the drawer and his fingers groped frantically for the key in his pocket. When a heavy sea surged into his room and banged him against the wall, Lumsden forgot the money and papers. He grabbed his lifebelt, and, half swimming, flailed this way to the cross-alleyway. Presently he reached the first-class section where the stairway leading to the boat deck was solidly blocked with people and luggage, all pushing upward to get away from the rising water.

Other survivors were straggling up the stairs from below. It was now eight or nine minutes since the *Florizel* had struck the reef.

She still had her lights and whistle, but she was a dying ship, almost completely flooded as the ocean poured through every opening and plunged into her belly. A few people were still below: Minnie Denief was trapped in the dining saloon, and perhaps Elizabeth Pelley. Old Mr. Connolly had drowned in his berth.

In the after part of the ship, Fagan and Fowlow saw the sea rushing into their room and leapt out of their berths. In the stern, Maloney, Crockwell, and young Guzzwell were battling the rising water, trying to find a way out. Terrified by the uproar, the boy was hysterical.

The majority of passengers were jammed in the stairway leading to the boat deck. Some had slipped outside and had been carried to the starboard rail. Of these, some made it to the lee of the smoker and held on to the smoker handrailing; others were swept overboard to their death. Several were in the smoker, quaking and shivering in pajamas and jacket; very few were fully clad. The ship's stewards and engineers, huddled in the companionway with the passengers, were helpless to do anything.

The Spanish firemen had assembled on the boat deck beside one of the lifeboats, and seamen were already in the act of cutting the coverings. Major Sullivan was in the lee of the smokestack, and Marconi operator John Bernard Murphy was trying to reach the bridge to find out the ship's position as Carter tapped out the s.o.s.

The number-one lifeboat was on the starboard side immediately aft of the captain's cabin and Jackman, Dooley, Gover, Power, and Pinsent were struggling to free it when a giant wave built up and towered over the *Florizel*. Up, up above her port quarter it rose, as high as the topmast and the funnel. The ship lay still; an eerie quiet prevailed as the giant wave blocked wind and sound, then it curled over, crashing upon her deck with a roar. The lifeboats were torn from the davits on the port side and flung across the deck to smash down on the lifeboats on the starboard side.

The sailors were washed about the deck, frantically clawing at anything that came to hand to keep from going overboard. Some were taken over the side.

Aft of the smokestack on the port side, the steel lifeboat, still in its chocks, was torn from the deck, carried over the smokestack, and dropped athwart the deck between the broken skylight over the social hall and the starboard rail. There it stayed, securely jammed.

Captain Kean was hit by a piece of wreckage and, with a broken leg and bleeding head, was swept toward the rail on the starboard side.

At the same time the whistle stopped and the *Florizel* suddenly was plunged into darkness.

# CHAPTER 12

*THE LIGHTS* did not flicker or give warning, they simply went out. Whether the steam was exhausted or the water had flooded the dynamo, the *Florizel* was suddenly in total darkness.

On deck, Mate James grabbed Captain Kean as he slid toward the rail, and with the help of Seaman Dooley dragged him to the sheltered side of the captain's cabin. "Are you all right?" he yelled.

Joe gasped: "My leg is broken."

Another wave was building, rearing big and ugly above the port quarter, and crew members were still floundering about the deck. James left Captain Kean and hauled some of them to the shelter of the superstructure before the giant sea rolled over.

By some mysterious phenomenon of nature, seas like that came in threes, approximately twenty seconds apart, and the seamen, being aware of it, dashed for what protection they could find before the next wave came. Each one took a number of passengers and crew members overboard.

Major Sullivan, still in the shelter of the smokestack

when the first wave smashed the lifeboats, could see men helping men, dragging dazed sailors from the open deck to the smokestack or the captain's cabin. He dashed across the boat deck to the forward superstructure where he hung on, with others, until the second and third giant waves passed. The sheen from the white water made it appear lighter than it actually was, and he found his way to the captain's cabin where many of the seamen were regrouping for further orders. Several passengers were there, too, including William Parmiter and John Connolly.

It was here that wireless operator Bernard Murphy found the captain. Murphy had been blundering around the empty wheelhouse and chartroom in the darkness shouting for the captain, and had finally clattered down the ladder to the captain's cabin where Martin was passing out lifebelts.

"What's our position, Cap'n? Mr. Carter wants to know," he yelled.

Martin replied, "Near Cape Race."

Murphy pounded back to the Marconi room. "We're ashore near Cape Race," he panted.

Carter, holding a flashlight, was already tapping out the s.o.s. on the key. The current from the dynamo had failed with the first big sea and he had switched to the auxiliary set.

"S.O.S.! S.O.S.! S.O.S.! *Florizel*. Ashore near Cape Race. Fast going to pieces."

He did not stop transmitting to await a reply but, hunched tensely over the little fingerpiece, kept on sending the message. After three minutes there was no spark from the emergency apparatus. The set was dead.

"That's it!" Carter said with finality. "The aerial must be down."

The water was rushing around the smokestack, smashing into the Marconi house, which shook in the

*The S.S.* Florizel, *transporting 540 men of the First Newfoundland Regiment overseas in October, 1914. Joseph Maloney is aboard.*

*The wreck of the* Florizel. *The smokestack protected the Marconi house, but the boat deck collapsed under the giant seas.*

*The port side took the brunt of the sea. Note the crushed side of the social hall, the collapsed deck, and the steel plating rolled back.*

*A view of the fiddley (A) and the Marconi house (B), where survivors huddled. The fishermen of Cappahayden and nearby communities strip the wreck.*

Captain William J. Martin, a careful and prudent master, ran his ship upon a reef.

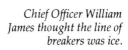

Chief Officer William James thought the line of breakers was ice.

Third Officer Philip Jackman spent an uneasy night.

(Top left) *Second Engineer Thomas Lumsden was on duty when the Florizel struck.* (Top right) *Third Engineer Eric Collier thought the ship would not sail until the storm passed.* (Lower left) *Wireless operator Cecil Sidney Carter sent out the S.O.S.* (Lower right) *Wireless operator Bernard John Murphy watched men tumble about the deck.*

(Right) *Fourth Engineer Herbert Taylor was swept overboard three times.* (Lower left) *John Johnston, pantry waiter, heroically saved Minnie Denief.* (Lower right) *Oiler Edward Timmons heard trapped women screaming.*

*Lieutenant Ralph Burnham was a cripple for life after the wreck.*

*Gregory Maloney escaped through the skylight.*

*Major Michael Sullivan had to be towed through angry seas to the lifeboat.*

*Dave Griffiths was carried from the smoker to the bridge by heavy seas.*

*John Cleary warded off danger with his crucifix.*

*John Kieley sought shelter in the wardrobe in his room.*

(Top) *Minnie Denief outside her home in Brooklyn, N.Y., 45 years after the disaster. (She had sailed for New York one year later.)*
(Below) *Kitty Cantwell, 45 years after the wreck. She never set foot aboard a ship again.*

most frightening manner. Carter yelled, "We'd better get out of here."

Once outside, they had to grab the handrail around the outside of the wireless house to keep from being swept away. They had no idea where safety lay, but they had no confidence in the little Marconi house. In the light cast by the boiling surf, they could see the ship disintegrating around them, and it was obvious that no lifeboat could live in the seas tumbling over the reef that trapped the *Florizel*.

The lights went out as Stockley and Bartlett were scrambling up over the stairway that would take them to the deck behind the cargo winches of number-three hold. They made it topside, ran across the deck, and raced up the ladder to the boat deck. They ducked around to the lee of the smoker just as the second wave hit, taking Stockley's cap and muffler. The shock of the icy sea on his body took his breath away, but he and Bartlett made it safely. Clinging to the handrail, they were able to see the dim forms of several other people huddling there.

Maloney and Crockwell, with young Guzzwell, floundered on into the stern in the darkness. "There's a stairs back here somewhere," Maloney called out.

Their way was suddenly blocked by a torrent of water spilling in front of them. When the sea had passed over, Maloney peered upward. "It's the skylight!"

In spite of the dark the stern skylight was clearly outlined. That was their way out, the men decided. Maloney was of average height but of a muscular build and in good trim at one hundred and eighty pounds. On the other hand, Crockwell, though well over six feet, was bulkier and less physically fit at two hundred and forty pounds. It was decided that Maloney, with an assist from Crockwell, would go first.

It was no sooner said than done. With a heft from Crockwell, Maloney made a grab for the skylight combing and hauled himself on deck. Kneeling, he extended an arm below, but a sea swept him to the rail. Two passengers caught by the same wave, were carried overboard. As soon as he had collected his wits, Maloney lunged back to the skylight and poked his head inside. "Jim!" he bellowed. "Where are you?"

There was no reply. Crockwell and Billy Guzzwell were no longer beneath the skylight. Again Maloney yelled to Crockwell, but there was no answering shout. Another wave broke over the port quarter, and he dashed for the boat deck and the shelter of the smoker.

In the lamp room, Burry and Lambert considered themselves reasonably safe. Then the first wave hit the bulkhead, smashing the large porthole with such force that the glass projected like a missile across the tiny room, barely missing them. The ocean roared in and split the door, sweeping Burry and Lambert outside and forward into the bow, slamming them against the steel plates. Then the sea pulled back and they caught at the door frame and dragged themselves into the lamp room again. Lambert was in shock when the next wave swept them outside a second time. It flung him against the windlass and crushed his skull. Burry, nearly drowned, retained enough presence of mind to make a grab for the broken doorway and haul himself inside as the sea fell back. A short length of rope floated by, and he grabbed it, tied it around his waist, and lashed himself to a stanchion.

The faint light revealed a disturbingly familiar shoreline

to Philip Jackman. Sometime within the last ten minutes, the rain had stopped and he could see enough of it to recognize the contours of Horn Head and Burnt Head. His birthplace was Renews, a mere six miles away. *The* Florizel *had been steaming for over nine hours and had come to grief less than fifty miles from port.*

He knew now why it had been a rough voyage. The storm was only a moderate one, but they must have been steaming directly over, or very near, the Bantems; the shallow fishing grounds had caused the swells heaving in from the Atlantic to build steeply and create great turbulence as they rolled landward.

He knew exactly where they were. The *Florizel* had struck the ugly mass of rocks that ran two hundred and fifty yards out under the sea from Horn Head. On either side of the reef the water was deeper; southward of it was a comparatively quiet little cove. If she had cleared the reef she would have grounded much closer to land and their chances for survival would have been greater. As it was, *God help them!*

Captain Martin's face was a blur in the darkness. "Everyone will get their lifebelts!" he ordered, and turning to Jackman: "See that the passengers get lifebelts, Jackman."

The third officer snapped back to attention. "Yes, Cap'n."

There were two boxes of lifebelts on the deck aft of the smoker, and two boxes on each side of the fiddley casing, but to face the seas tumbling across the deck was madness. Jackman would have to get to the passengers through the social hall.

With the silencing of the whistle, the seas thundering around the ship filled the sound gap with terrifying effect. For the first time the passengers in the stairway were aware of the great peril in which they had been placed: the ship could not withstand such horrendous battering for very long.

Until now they had been frightened but well behaved; now there was panic, with those at the bottom of the stairway struggling to get away from the seas encroaching from below. Those near the top were equally anxious to escape the black confines of the companionway, but they could not move. John and Mary Maloney and baby John were there; Mary and the baby were crying.

From below a man bellowed, "We've got to get out of here or we'll drown like rats!"

There was another surge of pressure from the crowd. "Stop pushing!" a voice cried from the middle of the stairway. "The stairs are jammed with suitcases."

"To hell with the bloody suitcases, let us out of here!"

"We can't move, dammit," someone else roared angrily.

More angry voices joined in the altercation. It did not matter. Come what may, those below were determined to get out, and they pressed steadily upward. It worked. The pressure lessened up front as, one by one, passengers stepped out on deck and were carried to the starboard rail or swept overboard. Alex Ledingham was one of them. He found himself in the lee of the smoker, hanging to the handrail with a group of people.

J. P. Kieley did not hestitate when the lights went out; he went into his room and stayed there. Margaret Keough went with him.

In the starboard alleyway, Kitty Cantwell and Annie Dalton thrashed about in the darkness. Annie, shocked into a realization of what was happening, shrieked, "Kitty! Don't leave me!"

"I'm here," Kitty shouted, firmly grasping her friend;

then the sea lifted them off their feet. Carried first in one direction, then another, Kitty found herself at times on her knees, shoulder deep in the icy sea, clinging to a handrail or a door frame. Other passengers were crying out in fear, but Kitty conserved her energy, thinking, "Now what's the use of making all that noise?"

The darkness magnified the horror of their predicament. She had no knowledge of the ship, did not know where they should go for safety. Annie clung to her with ferocious strength. "Kitty, don't leave me," she gasped over and over.

Then Kitty's arms were locked around the stair post and they were in amongst the other survivors. She shoved through the crowd, pulling Annie behind her. In a few minutes they were on deck.

In the gray light Kitty had a brief glimpse of seas rolling toward her. With a roar the wall of black ocean struck the ship and she was aware only that she was clinging to the railing, staring at the black rocks showing briefly through the surf. Ugly and evil they looked, and so close that she thought she was right out amongst them. Terror caused her to black out. She came to, to find herself on the roof of the smoker with a number of other survivors, whipped by wind and sea. How she got there she would never remember, but Annie was still with her.

Those trapped below fought for survival in the dark. To battle the power of seas confined in the hull required every ounce of strength, courage, and will power of which a human was capable. With remarkable control, Fagan and Fowlow groped along the alleyway. Due to the starboard list, the water was not as deep on the port side as yet, but it was up to Fagan's thighs and climbing steadily. They found the stairway leading to the promenade deck a veritable waterfall, but, hearing the shouting of voices above, plunged through the torrent and fought upward into the group of people jammed together on the stairway.

Minnie Denief had to struggle against the rising waters in pitch blackness, but a fierce determination to live kept her moving in the direction of the grand stairway. Fighting with a tenacity that belied her frail appearance, she had no time to think of Elizabeth Pelley; but above her, Edward Timmons, making his way through the social hall to the alleyway aft, heard the screams of more than one woman tearing up through the opening.

Minnie was on her feet one minute, drowning the next, until battered and bruised, she found herself clinging to the stair railing. With thankful heart, she hauled herself up the stairs, hanging on for dear life when the seas fell over her, and reached the social hall. If she had not been so blind without her glasses, the devastation there might have demoralized her completely; as it was, the shouts and yells of the survivors aft guided her safely across the hall and through the alleyway. Presently she joined those clustered on the stairs.

Passengers huddled inside the smoker were miserably aware that their shelter was taking the brunt of the sea. The weather side was buckling, the doors had split, and the room was awash. The tarpaulin had been torn from the skylight and ice-cold spray fell on them constantly. Only a few passengers were fully dressed, others were barefooted in pajamas; a few wore dressing gowns. It was a wretched place to be, and one by one they slipped outside to find better shelter. The deck was icy, and some, blown by the wind, skidded wildly down the sloping deck to be washed overboard before they knew what had happened. The more cautious ones grabbed the handrail and eased themselves to the lee of the smoker.

A large group had already gathered there, and the first-class passengers edged through them to the front, with the intention of going forward to the bridge. The sight that greeted their eyes was a formidable one. Between them and the smokestack the sea fell madly upon the broken engine-room skylight; the cowls of two ventilators gaped at them like monstrous vacant eyes. Wreckage had piled up on the starboard side and bodies rolled about in the combers sluicing over the deck.

It stopped them in their tracks. Beside them a steel ladder went up to the smoker roof, and as the seas reached for them they climbed hastily to the roof. Some of these passengers had spent many pleasant hours sunning on top of the smoker during her trips; this time they were at the cold mercy of the wind and sea. John Munn and a light-haired woman* were among those who sought refuge there.

Almost imperceptibly it was growing light. The moon, which had remained hidden throughout the crucial hours of night, now peeked briefly through scudding storm clouds. Very few noticed it.

The passengers in the companionway made the horrifying discovery that many of the people were being swept overboard as they stepped outside. In fright and shock, those inside barred the door, yelling, "Don't go out there! Get back!"

Not understanding, the crowd below shoved harder. "We'll drown if you don't let us out of here. Open the door!"

"You might as well drown in here as out there," someone shouted from above.

"What do you mean?"

* Thought to be Evelyn Trenchard.

"Don't you understand? Everybody who goes out there is swept away," a voice yelled. "Lost!"

The information was passed through the crowd, but it didn't matter. A grim struggle began. The pressure from below increased as the survivors pushed steadily upward and those above resisted.

Lumsden, Collier, Taylor, Timmons, Joseph Moore, and Dave Griffiths were there, and on the bottom step, behind the crowd, Minnie Denief clung to the handrail. Somewhere in the jam of people the Maloney family clung together, the baby still crying. George Moulton and young Clarence were there too.

Regardless of the warning that to go outside was to perish, Dave Griffiths felt that as long as he knew what to expect, his chances were much better outside. Certain death awaited them in the companionway, whereas on deck there was a fighting chance.

He worked his way upward through the crowd, managed to open the door, and slipped outside. Before he could get his bearings, a heavy swell engulfed him. The icy sea penetrated his overcoat, struck his skin like ice-fire, and left him gasping. He hit the starboard rail and clung to it, and then, like others before him, reached for the smoker handrail. He could see dim forms huddled there, and he pulled himself to the forward end. The scene of devastation was so awful that he turned from it and climbed to the roof of the smoker to join the forlorn group of people there.

Alex Ledingham had not remained in the lee of the smoker with other passengers, but had dashed past the wreckage, clambered over the steel lifeboat athwart the deck, and reached the shelter of the superstructure.

In the lee of the captain's cabin, he found Chief Steward Charlie Snow with a terrified Betty Munn clinging to his neck. To Ledingham's mind they were as safe there as anywhere. He did not speak to Snow, but ran up the ladder to the bridge and wheelhouse. Captain Martin was in the chartroom with Major Sullivan, who was tying on a lifebelt, and Ledingham asked, "Is there anything I can do, Captain?"

Martin replied, "There's nothing you can do, Alex, except try and find a place to hang on."

Jackman, meanwhile, reached the social hall, which was a complete wreck. Tables, chairs, and sofas, wrenched from their floor moorings, had piled up against the starboard wall; the railing was gone from the stairway and the circular hole above the dining saloon, and the sea was pouring into the interior of the ship. The windows had smashed and the wind knifed in. Jackman knew that the *Florizel* was finished.

He plowed aft through the port alleyway, guided by the cries of the survivors, and found them huddled in the stairway — dim, formless shapes in the pre-dawn light. Their fear was a palpable thing. A child was crying, but the people were not too hysterical. Jackman moved up the stairs amongst them, uttering soothing words of reassurance. "Don't panic, the main thing is not to panic," he kept saying over and over.

They recognized the voice of authority and were comforted, thinking it was the captain. "Does everyone have lifebelts?" Jackman asked.

Very few of them did.

"There might be lifebelts on deck: *If there are*, I'll pass them to you, but you *must* try and get forward to the bridge," he cautioned.

No one at this time seemed anxious to leave the shelter of the companionway, and with further admonitions about going forward, Jackman slipped through the battered door and grabbed for the handrail as the sea rushed at him in the grayness of false dawn.

The boxes containing the lifebelts had been swept away, he noted. Also, the weatherside of the smoker was disintegrating steadily; the whole after part of the ship was under water and sinking steadily. Hearing the cries and groans of survivors in the lee of the smoker, he worked his way over to them. There seemed to be no ship's personnel to assist them on deck.

Jackman urged them to try and get forward; they did not heed his words. He then climbed to the roof of the smoker, where he found about forty more survivors clinging to the railing.

Jackman yelled, "You'll all have to try and get to the bridge; it's safer there."

They appeared to be made of stone. From where they stood, the scene below was one of total destruction and it seemed unreasonable to expect them to descend into it, but Jackman knew the danger of their present position. He repeated his warning, but still no one moved. Then John Munn's voice came out of the noise and confusion: "Is that you, Jackman?"

Jackman recognized the voice. "Mr. Munn! Are you all right?"

They moved toward each other. John Munn's face was a pale blur.

"Where are we, Jackman; where did we run ashore?"

Jackman hesitated to put into words where he thought they were, but John Munn waited. "It looks like Horn Head, but we've been steaming such a long time it *can't* be Horn Head."

"What do you think, Jackman; can the *Florizel* stand this?" Munn asked as another wave broke over the ship.

Jackman had every confidence in the sturdy *Florizel* on the water; rocks were a different matter. He shouted back, "I think the hull is good for it, sir. The only thing we can do is try to hang on until help arrives."

"Yes," Munn replied. "I lost Betty, Jackman. I had her in my arms and the sea took her from me as I was crossing the deck."

Jackman had not known that little Betty was on board, and said so.

Munn lifted a bare foot and rubbed it, seemingly oblivious of the bitter cold. "I have no boots. Do you know where I can get a pair?"

"Take mine, Mr. Munn." Jackman bent over to remove his own boots.

Munn halted him. "I don't want your boots, Jackman, but see if you can find another pair." He added in a broken voice, "Though I don't much care what happens to me after losing Betty."

"You've got to get forward, Mr. Munn." Jackman then appealed to the other passengers again: "Everybody should try and get forward; it's safer there."

John Munn disagreed. The smoker was part of the steel superstructure of the ship and it would stand. "I think it's as safe here as it is forward," he said, "so I'll stay here."

The majority followed Munn's leadership and remained on the roof with him. Only a few left, slipping down the ladder and leaping over wreckage and bodies on the deck to reach the safety of the smokestack.

Munn remained adamant to Jackman's last plea, and looking at the devastation around them, at the seas smashing against the smokestack and the bridge, Jackman felt, too, that perhaps the passengers were as safe here as they were anywhere. Anyway, he could not make them move if they did not choose to do so.

He left the roof and returned to the survivors clinging to the smoker handrail below. "You'll have to go forward," he shouted, indicating the way where they must go, but they too refused to budge.

And suddenly Jackman decided to stay with them.

127

*THE STERN* of the *Florizel* had disappeared beneath the furious seas, the after part was sagging badly from amidships, the promenade deck from the social hall back was under water, and a number of survivors were still in the companionway, gathering courage for that dash outside.

Lumsden, Collier, Taylor, Timmons, and Davis left, one behind the other, and reached the smoker. Others were following when a monstrous wall of water rose high above the port quarter and then rolled inexorably forward. It hit the superstructure, buckled the weather side of the smoker, shattered the door of the companionway leading to the first-class accommodations, and swept on to engulf the smokestack and the bridge. Several passengers disappeared from the smoker roof, people were washed overboard and back again.

Dave Griffiths felt as if the life was being squeezed out of him when the wave hit. It sucked the air from his lungs and snatched his hat from his head. Catching his breath, he saw it perched incongruously on the rail to his right and — recklessly — he dashed for it.

John Munn still clung to the rail while the woman close to him cried, "Save me!"

Munn replied, "I cannot do anything for myself; I cannot do anything for you."

The second giant wave rolled over, and when it had passed, Dave's hat was gone, this time for good. So were a few more passengers. The third wave diminished their group further.

Those survivors in the companionway had held their breath as the first wave was building; that momentary eerie quiet was ominous. As it struck, a voice yelled, "The door is split! *Watch out!*"

The door shattered inward and the water flooded into the companionway, carrying all before it. Down over the stairs and back into the alleyways went the people, their shouts and screams fading to gasps and gurgles. Minnie Denief was amongst them. Above the frightful din she heard a woman scream; then she was fighting the water as it pulled her under and filled her stomach as she gasped for air — but there was no air and she was drowning. Then, quite clearly, an inner voice commanded, "Get up! You are not going to drown!"

She thumped into a wall and some dim spark in her brain sent her hands groping. They closed around the railing in the alleyway, and suddenly she was able to breathe again. Life flowed back into her body as she hung on, spewing salt water.

She stayed there collecting her wits as the next two waves hit, and when the water quietened in the alleyway, she made her painful way back to the stairs. Through salt-bleared eyes she could see the patch of dim light where the door had been. There seemed to be nobody around. Had everybody drowned?

As she reached the top of the stairs, she saw a man clinging to the railing just inside the opening. "Help me!" she implored.

"Is that you, Miss Denief?" It was John Johnston.

"Yes!" It was a cry of thankfulness that someone knew her. "Yes, it's me."

He extended an arm. "Here, grab my hand."

She grabbed, and Johnston yelled, "Grab hold of my lifebelt!"

Obediently, Minnie hooked her arm through Johnston's lifebelt. "We've got to get out of here," he shouted. "When I move, you move. Hang on, and *don't let go!*"

In the brief moment before the next sea engulfed them, Minnie saw a man and woman appear on the deck beside them, saw them carried away. When it passed, Johnston shouted, *"Now!"* Clutching the handrail, he pulled himself and Minnie around the after end of the smoker and joined the others huddled there.

Passenger William Moore was there, fully dressed; so were the engineers, the stewards as well as other passengers and crew members. Herbert Taylor, battered, bruised and half drowned by the three giant waves that had carried him overboard and swept him back each time, was somehow managing to cling dazedly to the rail.

Joseph Moore, the lanky second cook, was among the group of people hurtled back into the ship when the wave split the companionway door. He could hear the terrified cries of passengers as they were flung around the alleyways. Stateroom furniture and other wreckage added to the hazards of survival.

Moore kept his head, letting the seas take him where they would, and presently he came to a stop in less turbulent, comparatively shallow waters in a cross-alleyway. He was taller than average and his height stood him in good stead: when the sea settled down it was not too bad, though at times it surged up to his shoulders. He anchored himself at the handrail so that he could catch his breath and get his bearings. As gray daylight filtered in through the broken ship Moore was able to take stock of his surroundings. Although the after end was now almost completely underwater, for the time being there seemed to be some measure of safety in the cross-alleyway.

He saw that he was immediately aft of the social hall, and facing him was Room 19, recently occupied by Kitty Cantwell and Annie Dalton. The door was open and he took a look inside; a girl* was there, crouched in the upper berth, frozen with terror. She said nothing, offered no information as to who she was, and Moore, his senses shocked, did not ask. Moments later a man and a young boy were swept into the alleyway, struggling feebly against the current. Moore dragged them, half dead, from the wreckage. They were in no condition to take care of themselves, and he assisted them into Room 19 where the young girl was. "You'll be all right in here," he told them.

Man and boy,† obviously in the last stages of exhaustion, collapsed on the berth.

Moore did more exploring and received another surprise. Room 2 had an occupant. Stewardess Margaret Keough was kneeling in the upper berth, straining to see through the window. Huge white-crested combers were smashing against the glass and reverberating thunderously on the steel plating of the ship. Miss Keough was frightened but collected. "Mr. Kieley is in the closet," she said, pointing.

"Did you say something, Miss Keough?" The closet door swung open and Moore looked up at the portly figure of John Kieley wedged in on the top shelf. Kieley held the end of a cord, used to tie back the berth cur-

---

* Probably the blind girl, Blanche Beaumont.
† Undoubtedly George Moulton and his son Clarence.

tains, in one hand; the other end was tied to the door knob. As the sea surged into the room, Kieley hauled the door to, when the seas receded, he let the door swing open. "It keeps the closet dry," he explained gravely.

They were all safe for the time being, but trapped in the hull.

Although the smoker roof was splitting and sagging, thirty or more passengers were still there, ill clad and huddled together in the early dawn. How they survived for any length of time — why they had not been overwhelmed by the sheer brute force of the ocean — was a miracle in itself; but as each wave passed, their number diminished.

The large group of crew and passengers in the lee of the smoker were petrified with fear and could only cling to whatever came to hand. Mary Maloney, cowering against her husband, sobbed: "Pray. Our only hope is to pray."

They were too numbed to pray. The deck beneath their feet was treacherously icy. Spume stung their flesh like needles, the wind made their bones ache — only their hands appeared to have the life and will to hang on, to obey the blind instinct to survive. Jackman had seen a woman, dressed only in a nightgown, hanging straight out over the side of the ship. No man near her had offered a helping hand and she had been swept away.* "You'll *have* to make a run for it," he bawled. "The after part is sinking, *you'll have to go forward.*"

Gunner George Curtis† was also urging the people forward: "The bow is higher; it's safer there."

* Revealed in an interview with Mary Jackman.
† Curtis was the only man to testify that Chief Reader was with this group of survivors.

Gradually the passengers bestirred themselves. No one could rig lifelines for them because there were none; they were on their own. To set an example, Curtis dashed toward the bow. Leaping over the wreckage, he darted around the smokestack and then dashed inside the fiddley casing. He found a handful of Spanish firemen huddled together on the grating over the stokehold. Curtis did not stay there long; he rushed for the Marconi house, five or six feet away, yelling to the wireless operators, Carter and Murphy, to get inside. They did so, but with little faith that the little structure would last.

Finally, others survivors began to leave the smoker, and those who made it safely to the smokestack made a beeline for the Marconi house, squeezing thankfully inside. Among them were Edward Timmons and John Davis.

The bridge was awash. In the chartroom, Captain Martin opened the wooden box where signal lights were kept, and was examining them with the aid of Sullivan's flashlight.

"Can we raise a signal?" Sullivan asked hopefully.

Martin replied, "We can try, but they're wet."

Ledingham had joined them and the three men tried unsuccessfully to light the rockets. "They won't work," Martin said at last.

It was gradually brightening and Martin cast about to see what, if anything, could be done. Great running combers were twisting the superstructure; spume and water flew across the deck in drenching sheets. The ship was completely flooded below deck; the hatch of number-two hold had floated free and casks of fish were tumbling over the starboard side. Survivors still remained on the smoker roof aft; about twenty were clinging to anything they could find in the wheelhouse.

Martin saw all too clearly that there was nothing he, or anyone, could do.

Hearing cries on the deck beneath the bridge, Martin descended by the still intact starboard ladder. Ledingham followed. One of the passengers said with great feeling, "Captain, you have my sympathy." It was James Miller, whose father was the chief steward of the S. S. *Prospero*, (another of Bowring's Red Cross Line). As a member of a seafaring family, he knew of the trials ahead for Captain Martin if he survived.

Martin saw Joe Kean for the first time; Joe was crumpled on the deck, bleeding profusely from a wound on the head. Martin shouted, to no one in particular, "Give me a hand with Captain Kean."

Kean said, "My leg is broken."

Ledingham and Mate James each took an arm, Martin lifted him by his good leg, and they eased the fainting man up the steep ladder to the wheelhouse and placed him on a locker. Somebody produced a handkerchief and they staunched the wound, tying the cloth around his head. Martin went to the chartroom, brought out an old cap, and placed it on Joe's head. "It's the best I can do," he said.

"Thank you," Kean murmured.

As they looked toward the shore, they were now able to see the men of Cappahayden staring helplessly at the *Florizel*.

"If you have oil on board it would quieten the sea and give the men ashore a chance to get to us," Sullivan suggested.

Martin said flatly, "We do have oil, Major, but it's in the hold and my men can't possibly get at it."

The people still outside the smoker found themselves in ever-worsening straits as the stern sank lower and lower. One by one they abandoned their position, each

134

survivor gauging the seas to the best of his ability, and following the example of the ones gone before, dashed for the relative safety of the smokestack. Jimmy Dwyer received a crack on the shin as he dodged through the wreckage; several passengers were swept overboard as they tried to skirt it. Others, caught by the sea, had the presence of mind to grab the combing of the skylight; guy-ropes and wire stays supporting the smokestack were still intact and came to hand for those who were alert enough to grasp them. Very few did.

Stockley and Bartlett had seen many passengers disappear overboard. Finally Stockley yelled to Bartlett, "I'm going for'ard. You coming, Cap?"

Bartlett yelled back, "Look out for your*self*, Jim; I'll be all right."

"You sure?"

"Look out for yourself."

Beside them, Joseph Maloney held his infant son in one arm; his wife clung to the other. She was praying with fervor.

Waiting for the break between waves, Stockley rushed forward in leaps and bounds; he had barely reached the smokestack when a sea flung him to the deck. Stockley thought he was finished, but his hands grabbed one of the wires supporting the smokestack and he held on as he was washed about the deck. Then the danger was past and he scurried around the smokestack, saw the Marconi house, and dashed for it. He pounded on the door, pushed it open, and squeezed inside.

Herbert Taylor, still outside the smoker, heard a woman cry out, ":Will you help me?"

It was Mabel Barrett, wearing only a dressing gown over her nightdress, drenched and in an exhausted condition. Taylor croaked, "Hang on to my arm, Miss Barrett, I'll do the best I can."

As she took his arm, Herbert, sick from swallowing sea water, knew he could not take the punishment of wind and sea much longer. "We'll have to go forward," he told her. As they were inching cautiously forward, still in the lee of the smoker, another sea rolled over them. When it passed, Mabel Barrett was no longer at his side. Taylor shouted her name, but there was no sign of her.

Mabel Barrett was still alive. She had been swept forward and around to the front of the smoker, where she had grasped the ladder leading to the roof. Dazed, she sat on the steps, wrapping her arms around the rail. Dave Griffiths, still on the roof, saw her clinging to the ladder and thought, "I can't help you now, Mabel Barrett." He had barely sent the thought when the second wave bore down on them. It sucked Mabel from the ladder. Dave watched her being driven along the deck, screaming; saw her head hit a piece of torn metal and the blood gush out. He could only hang on as the third wave struck, but Mabel Barrett was already dead and washing around the deck.

Beside him, John Munn stooped to squeeze his bare feet. "My feet," he muttered, "my feet."

The smoker was gradually collapsing, sinking with the rest of the after part of the ship, and Dave knew he had to get out of there if he hoped to survive. He knew this, but still he clung to the railing.

Joseph Maloney decided it was time to get his wife and child forward to safety, "Be ready when I say," he commanded Mary. He studied the seas. "Now!" he yelled, and they dashed forward.

But he was burdened with a baby and a frightened woman, the wreckage had to be skirted or jumped over, which required split-second timing. A wave lifted over the bulwark, threw them to the deck, swept them toward the wreckage. When the sea passed, Mary and the baby were gone.

Dazed, Maloney clung to the railing, the wind and sea flaying his body.

He remained there a long time, staring blankly out over the angry waters.

In the lee of the smoker, Mr. and Mrs. William Butler, long separated from Henry Dodd and their precious black bag, now found themselves next to James McCoubrey, Mrs. Butler's brother-in-law.

Butler called out to McCoubrey, "We'd better get forward, everybody else is going there."

"Right!" McCoubrey shouted back. To his sister-in-law he said, "Give me your hand."

McCoubrey and her husband took her hands, and, gauging the seas to the best of their ability, they made the rush forward, but were caught in the swell and carried away, still holding hands.

Edward Berteau, in pajamas and overcoat, made it to the Marconi house but was swept overboard before he could get inside.

Ralph Burnham, fully dressed, also made the dash for safety. He hurdled the debris but was lifted off his feet and slammed against the sea rail into a niche miraculously devoid of wreckage. His eye caught sight of a round cork life preserver tied to the rail beside him; but before he could grab it, it was whipped overboard and the ropes that had secured it writhed in the wind. Burnham snatched the rope ends and lashed himself securely to the rail.

For the time being he was safe.

Lumsden, Collier, and Taylor decided it was time to go forward. There was no sign of Chief Reader. One after another they reached the smokestack safely, pausing long enough to see the devastation before dashing into the fiddley. Hennebury and a handful of Spanish firemen were huddled together on the grating of the stokehold, now completely flooded.

The Marconi house was only a few feet away and Edward Timmons, just inside the door, shouted to them, "Come on in here, boys." It was wet and drafty in the fiddley, and Collier and Hennebury decided to join him in the wireless house.

They had barely stepped outside when a wave crashed over the smokestack. Hennebury grabbed Collier, who was in the lead; Lumsden grabbed Hennebury and hauled both of them back inside.

The erratic movements of the ship as the seas worked her over made it precarious for survivors even in the protection of the fiddley. Suddenly, with a grating screech, the funnel began to slide downward as the boilers tore through the bottom of the ship.

There was panic. "The fiddley's sinking!"

All scrambled for the opening.

Lumsden shouted, "Wait! It's all right!"

He had noted that although the funnel had dropped, the fiddley had not. The iron grating on which they stood was not attached to the smokestack, but was part of the structure of the deck.

The *Florizel* shuddered violently, then began to rattle back and forth: with the boilers and the smokestack detached, the movements of the wreck grew wilder.

Hennebury made a decision. "I'm going to the Marconi house anyway," he said, and rushed out. A sea caught him and he vanished.

This effectively stopped anyone else from dashing the short distance to the little house, but the sea dripping continually on their heads became unendurable, and after a short time they ran, one after the other, across the deck to the Marconi house. Timmons let them in.

As other survivors crowded into the little room,

Joseph Stockley heard Captain Bartlett's voice. "Is that you, Cap?" he shouted.

Bartlett replied, "Yes, it's me." But he did not stay. He decided to go to the bridge so that he might be of some help to Captain Martin.

Philip Jackman had gone forward to the bridge, but John Johnston and Minnie Denief still hugged the smoker rail. It seemed less dark now, and they appeared to be the only ones left. Minnie, in her thin sweater, did not feel the cold. She did not feel anything. Her long black hair was plastered to her body; her arms were hooked through Johnston's lifebelt.

Johnston shouted, "We'll have to go forward."

She trusted him implicitly. "All right."

At that moment a great wave knocked them off their feet and carried them to the sea rail, lifting Minnie over Johnston's head. He clutched the rail and hung on while Minnie, battered and drowning, clung to his lifebelt with a vise-like grip. Her body swung straight out over the boiling seas, but her arms did not release Johnston's lifebelt. Miraculously, the backward motion of the wave brought her in over the rail, Johnston's body broke the pull of the sea, and she settled to the deck, spewing sea water. He drew her to the shelter of the smoker where they rested briefly. "You're all right," he encouraged her.

But the smoker was buckling and splintering beneath the ravaging seas; the after end had disappeared completely. They had to move. Johnston shouted. "Are you ready to make a run for it?"

"Yes!" Minnie screamed.

"We'll make for the captain's cabin; it'll be safer there."

He waited for the next brief lull and then yelled, "Now!"

Johnston could have made it quickly and easily on his

own, but Minnie slowed him so that the next wave caught them near the engine-room skylight, lifting them both off their feet.

Involuntarily, Minnie let go of Johnston's lifebelt. A cry of terror died in her throat as she felt herself lifted by the sea. This was the end, her struggles had been in vain — her mind accepted this in an instant. But Johnston lunged for the skylight with his left hand and made a grab for her with the other. He caught her by her long black hair and twisted it around his fist.

Completely spent and half drowned, Minnie was unable to help herself. Johnston began to pull her across the deck by her hair, mouthing words of encouragement. It did not matter; she simply lay there. Johnston swiftly unwound his fist from her hair, transferred his grip to her ankle, and dragged her to the shelter of the smokestack. Here, he pulled her to her feet, rushed her across the slippery deck toward the captain's cabin, and was appalled to find that the shelter here was no better than the shelter they had left. The quarters of James and King, aft of the captain's cabin, were completely demolished, and Martin's cabin was also buckling under the constant pounding of the waves. Johnston took a long, hard look at the Marconi house, protected to some degree by the smokestack.

"Come along, Miss Denief, we'll try the Marconi house," he yelled, "Hang on and *don't let go.*"

Minnie would not remember, later, that they had made it to the bridge; she was aware only of being pushed into the wireless room and of being safe at last. Her eyes smarted with salt water, but she saw, dimly, that it was an incredibly small place, and already crowded. Johnston worked his way through the knot of people, opened the drawer under the bunk and hauled out a blanket. He folded it double and laid it over Minnie's head and shoulders. "You're all right now, Miss Denief," he said.

All the surviving stewards and engineers were there. Johnston noticed that Arch Gardiner was wearing a wrist watch and asked, "What time is it, sir?"

Gardiner checked. "Five past six."

An interminable hour and fifteen minutes had crawled by since the *Florizel* had struck.

Gradually, survivors found their way to the Marconi house, which soon filled to overflowing, so much so that they began to throw out everything movable. Even the shelves projecting from the wall were wrenched off with a hammer and tossed outside. So far, Minnie was the only female there. She was not aware that she had lost a considerable quantity of hair when Johnston had grabbed her.

Maloney staggered into the Marconi room. He wore only his singlet and pants, his eyes were wild. "I lost my wife and baby — they went overboard," he croaked. He was pushed into the crowd as other people tumbled in behind him, and Minnie found herself right next to him.

Noah Dauphinee and Captain Belleveau were among those passengers still on the roof of the smoker, although it was almost completely under water now. John Munn clung to the rail with a death-like grip, his body rigid. Tom McNeil, Wilbert Butler, James Baggs, and F. C. Smythe had been swept away long ago.

Suddenly Dauphinee heard Belleveau shout, "Here comes another!" He saw his captain disappear in the wall of water, and Dauphinee knew he had to get forward or die. He laid a stiff, cramped hand on John Munn's shoulder, yelling, "This is no place for us, we should get to the bridge."

Munn did not answer; he appeared to be like a man already dead, and Dauphinee did not waste any more precious seconds. He climbed the railing and dropped down to the boat deck. Slipping and sliding on the icy deck, he reached the smokestack and dodged into its protection. Noting the ominous quiet preceding the next onslaught, he grabbed the rungs going up the side of the fiddley casing and hung on as the second and third waves swept over. Then he dropped to the deck and sprinted for the bridge, leaping over the steel lifeboat to hurtle amongst the passengers and crew sheltering in the lee of the captain's cabin. He recognized Chief Steward Snow, but there was no sign of Betty Munn.

Still lashed to the rail, pummeled by the waves, immersed for endless moments, Ralph Burnham was a spectator in the grim life-and-death struggle. Survivors came from everywhere, darting out of unlikely places to pound on the Marconi house door and force their way inside. Between seas he saw a survivor wrestle the overcoat off a dead body and put it on his own sparsely clad form. A few others followed suit.

To his horror, one of the bodies began to beat up against him. He made desperate attempts to avoid it, but could not.

It was too much. . . .

Annie Dalton and Kitty Cantwell clung wretchedly to the smoker railing. Kitty had turned up the big collar of her coat, holding her breath as each wave engulfed them. She did not know how long it had been since she and Annie had found themselves there; it was a nightmare of sound and fury in which time stood still and each moment was forever. Annie had stayed close, uttering no sound, her hands locked around the railing. The deck below was awash with wreckage and bodies rolling about like rag dolls. Every horrible detail was burned on Kitty's brain until she could absorb no more.

Presently she realized that only a handful of them

were still on the roof. As she watched, a man ran across the deck and disappeared behind the smokestack. It occurred to her that she had seen several others doing the same thing, and her brain began to function again. She and Annie had better move too.

She placed a cramped hand on her friend's arm. "Come on, Annie," she rasped, "we've got to get forward!"

Annie muttered, "I can't!"

"I'm going, Annie."

Her friend did not seem to hear.

"Annie!" It was a cry of desperation.

Annie was like one made of stone and Kitty knew she would have to leave her. "I'm going, Annie."

Stiffly, she started down the steep ladder to the boat deck. The water pulled at her with tremendous force as she clung to the rail. For the first time in her life, Kitty felt utterly alone. Suddenly a young man in khaki appeared out of nowhere; he seemed to have been brought there by the sea. Kitty immediately thought of Annie. "Can you look after my friend?" she implored. "She's up on the roof."

The man replied no, he could not, then a wave engulfed them and Kitty had to concentrate on surviving. When it passed, there was no sign of him.

She wasted no time; with her sodden clothes flapping around her legs, she scurried along the icy deck, past the splintered boats and twisted steel, and made it to the smokestack. There, before her eyes, was the small Marconi house. Although it looked less than safe, she knew instinctively that here was where the survivors were.

A wave struck Kitty and sent her tumbling along the deck, but her hand closed on a wire stay and she held on, smothering, until the water subsided. Then she scrambled to her feet and reeled toward the wireless house. She tried to push the door open but it was warped, so she pounded on the door. "Let me in! Let me in!"

A man's voice called back, "It's all filled in here."

"Let me in!" she cried again.

Another male voice behind the door bellowed, "Let the girl in!"

It took a moment or two, but the door opened protestingly and she was dragged inside. The tiny room was packed solidly with people and movement was difficult, but John Johnston was able to get another blanket out of the bunk drawer and drape it around Kitty's shoulders. Bernard John Murphy thoughtfully wrung out her hair.

CHAPTER *14*

THE FLORIZEL shuddered as the waves smashed against the smokestack and fell upon the Marconi house; combers, lifting over the port side, exploded against the forward structure, which was steadily breaking apart. The stern sagged more and more.

In the wheelhouse Major Sullivan was wedged behind the ship's wheel. Captain Joe Kean, wearing Captain Martin's cap over his bandage, sat quietly on the locker, his face gray with pain. Captain Martin, Second Officer John King, William Molloy, Michael Power, Charlie Snow, William Dooley, George Crocker, and passengers Alex Ledingham, James Miller, Jack Parsons, John Connolly, William Parmiter, John Cleary, and Paddy Fitzpatrick were among those grouped there. Parmiter asked Captain Kean point-blank, "Do you think we'll get out of this, sir?"

Kean replied, "If I had the use of my legs I might come out of it."

A wall of black ocean towered over the stern and spilled forward. It carried away the barricade, buckled and tore the weather side of the wheelhouse, forcing it over the superstructure to hang in a jagged, tangled mass above the foredeck. It smashed the wheel to bits, shattered the binnacle, and strewed debris around the wheelhouse. The survivors looked death squarely in the face as the second wave rolled over and flooded in through the gaping side. They spoke no word, uttered no sound, as the third wave went over, taking more of the wheelhouse but sparing them.

Captain Martin asked King, "Do you think the wheelhouse will stand?"

King was only vaguely comforting. "It'll probably stand for a little while, Cap." He added: "Help will be here soon."

"Yes," muttered the captain, "help will be here soon."

It sickened him to watch his ship disintegrating beneath his feet, but there was nothing mortal man could do. With a few words of encouragement to those around him, he went below.

The officers' cabins facing the smokestack were demolished, but the wreckage offered his own battered quarters a small measure of protection. Several passengers clung to the handrail around his cabin. "Keep your head," he told them. "Help will be here soon."

A few remained in the shattered wheelhouse, but the majority moved to the shelter of the starboard wing. Major Sullivan was one of them; he felt strongly that the whole superstructure was in danger. He joined Ledingham and some crew members who had taken refuge outside the captain's cabin. Others followed.

William Dooley and George Crocker remained in the wheelhouse. Staring at the rampaging ocean, Crocker said, "We're done for."

Dooley could not help but agree that the odds were stacked against their survival. "Maybe we should go below," he suggested.

"I don't think it would make any difference," Crocker said, adding "who'll look after Dora and the children?"

Dooley had no comforting words to offer Crocker. Instead, he said, "Let's go find the captain."

But Crocker decided to remain where he was. Dooley left the wheelhouse.

Philip Jackman had not forgotten the boots for John Munn, but the savage seas raking the *Florizel's* deck discouraged him from doing anything about it. He remained on the bridge with the other survivors. Joe Kean could not be moved; he remained on the locker, staring through the gaping side to the ugly seas beyond.

John Connolly and William Parmiter had stayed together. Connolly, only partially dressed, was suffering from shock and cold; Parmiter was fully dressed but without his overcoat. The view from the starboard wing was one continual scene of horror. Parmiter had seen a young soldier hanging in the rigging aft before the sea swept him away. Bodies floated about the deck, smashed against the ship's side, and he saw others, still living, lie on the bodies of the dead and permit themselves to be washed overboard. He watched as the passengers on the roof of the smoker were carried away one by one. Now, as their own group began to leave the bridge, Connolly and Parmiter followed suit.

Shelter below the bridge was no better. A wave surged around the captain's cabin, sweeping Parmiter to the sea rail. He wrapped his arms around a stanchion and hung on. When it passed he scuttled to the shelter of the cabin and went inside. The port wall had buckled, the port door was split and it offered very uncertain protection, but it was better than the raging deck outside.

Passengers Noah Dauphinee, Captain Bartlett, Alex Ledingham, Peter Guilfoyle, Major Sullivan, John Cleary, and Paddy Fitzpatrick were among the survivors hanging to the side of the cabin. A few went inside with Parmiter, but most stayed outside. About this time John Connolly slid to the deck and died.

Clinging to the rail around his cabin with these survivors, Captain Martin watched despairingly as his ship perished. The sea was a mass of white water over the sunken stern, and he wondered how long it would be before it tore away from the rest of the ship. Only the smoker roof remained above water and he could see that John Munn and a handful of others were still there. He knew that somehow he had to get aft and rescue them.

Martin clambered over the steel lifeboat and made a dash across the slippery deck. At that moment a huge wave rose high above the broken ship and spilled forward, carrying with it what was left of the smoker and the wheelhouse, taking with it John Munn, Captain Joe Kean, and about fifteen men, including Jack Parsons, Captain Bartlett, Paddy Fitzpatrick, Peter Guilfoyle, George Crocker, and Second Officer John King. Men and debris disappeared into the maelstrom of white surf. The second wall of ocean swept more men and flotsam before it; it smashed the captain's cabin and pinned Parmiter beneath the wreckage. Mate James, in the lee of the cabin, was pitched into a tangle of steel and wood. His hands closed around a stanchion, and he hung there as the third wave rolled over. Somehow he managed to haul himself, half drowned, back to the deck. The scene before him was even more desolate than before. The wheelhouse, chartroom, and bridge were gone; only the shattered captain's cabin and the steel lifeboat remained on the forward end of the boat deck. There was little, now, to protect those who had thus far survived.

Quartermaster Thomas Green was pinned beneath wreckage on the edge of the deck; his hands were broken and he could not free himself. Major Sullivan,

The battered little wireless house withstood the giant seas for 27 hours.
Inside, 34 survivors were crammed, awaiting rescue.

Eric Bowring, Director of
Bowring Brothers, Ltd.

The Honourable John Crosbie
organized the rescue operation.

*During the rescue a dory reached shore with the body of one of the victims.*

*A chair and table salvaged from the* **Florizel**. *Photo courtesy Mr. and Mrs. Thomas Williams.*

*The wreckage-strewn beach at Horn Head, Cappahayden.*

*Chief Engineer John Valder Reader said everything was all right in the engine room.*

*Second Officer John King was carried away by a giant wave.*

*George Crocker, a relief sailor, was on his last voyage.*

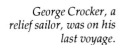

*John Shannon Munn,
Managing Director of the Red
Cross Line, was going to join his
wife in New York.*

*Captain Joe Kean had a broken
leg and a head wound.*

*James Crockwell was trapped in the stern.*

*Stormy weather changed the plans of James H. Baggs and placed him aboard the Florizel on her last voyage.*

*Clarence Moulton, a deaf mute, was on his way to school in Halifax.*

*Billy Guzzwell was joining his mother in New York.*

*Betty Munn, daughter of John S. Munn, was torn from her father's arms by heavy seas.*

*The statue of Peter Pan in Bowring Park erected in memory of little Betty Munn.*

also entangled, extricated himself in time to free Green and pull him to safety. He had to work furiously to free Green's boot from the jagged steel. William Molloy, pinned against the deck by the steel ladder that had led to the bridge, yelled to Dooley to help him. Dooley, who had been clinging to the captain's cabin, hauled the ladder away.

The third wave had swept the wreckage off Parmiter, but it had carried him again to the ship's sea rail, where he grabbed a stanchion and held on. When it passed, he crawled to the lee of what was left of the captain's cabin. The steel lifeboat, wedged firmly between the railing and the cabin, offered a little protection.

Philip Jackman was swept from the top bridge into the wreckage. He was knocked out briefly and came to on the edge of the deck. His nose was broken, cut, and hanging by the skin; his left cheek was gashed from the corner of his eye to his mouth, his upper lip split, his teeth knocked out and his shoulder dislocated. He scrambled to his feet, looked around, and saw that only the smokestack and the Marconi house were standing. He lurched toward the smokestack, as yet unaware of his injuries. He had it in mind to climb the iron ladder up the fiddley casing.

Dave Griffiths had been the last one on the roof with John Munn. He had seen the giant wave coming and yelled a warning. The next thing he knew, he was head down in the wreckage of the steel ladder. Dazed, he righted himself but was immediately thrown to the deck. Inexplicably, as though in a nightmare that skipped from scene to scene, he found himself overboard and drowning, but clinging to a rope; then he was washing about the deck just below the bridge. He heard a great tearing, crashing noise as the bridge went, and somehow he found himself in the wrecked half of a boat hanging from the davits. Beside him was a man who was bleeding profusely about the face. Groggily Dave asked, "Is it safe here?"

The man spoke, but Dave did not understand a word of what he was saying, then his mind went blank.

# CHAPTER 15

JOSEPH MOORE was exploring the area where he and the others were trapped below deck. He had to find a way out.

Because of the starboard list and the slope to the rear, the starboard alleyway was almost completely under water, although Room 18, in the forward section, looked as if it could still provide a degree of shelter. Was anybody in there? he wondered. A quick look showed a jagged hole in the outer wall through which the sea rushed and eddied. A sodden teddy bear on the upper berth was its only occupant.

The social hall was a great cavern of surging seas and floating wreckage, and it offered no way of escape. John Munn's room, however, was comparatively dry and offered the most security and the least discomfort. The survivors in Room 19 were still uncommunicative. Miss Keough and J. P. Kieley in Room 2 were more talkative.

Time dragged. Moore, continuing to check for possible escape routes, noticed that huge steam pipes crisscrossed the alleyways. They were not too close to the ceiling and being extremely thin, he was able to hoist himself upon them and worm his way along. The pipes either disappeared under the sea, aft, or went into the walls — there was no escape that way he realized.

Then he discovered that the boy in Room 19 was dead. Upset, he waded to Room 2 where he received a greater shock. The heavy square window had broken since his last visit, and Margaret Keough looked very strange, kneeling on the berth in an attitude of prayer, not flinching as the seas fell over her.

"Miss Keough!" he called.

From the wardrobe, Kieley asked, "How is Miss Keough? She's been pretty quiet."

Moore called her name again. When she did not move or reply, he touched her — and knew by the feel of her that no life remained in the still form. "She's dead!"

Kieley was unbelieving. "Dead? Are you sure?"

"I'm sure, Mr. Kieley."

"But she spoke to me a little while ago; she said daylight was breaking and rescue would soon be at hand, then the window broke and she got all wet." He was quite upset. "May the Lord have mercy on her soul!"

Moore did not touch her again. He told Kieley that there seemed to be no way of escape, and after a while left the room to check on the man and the girl in Room 19. He received another unpleasant surprise. The girl had disappeared.

"Where is she; what happened to her?" he asked the man.

The man did not answer. Moore shook him and knew instantly that *he was dead too!*

Where was the girl? Had the sea taken her? Or had panic sent her fleeing from the cabin?

Moore waded into the alleyway, frantically searching for some sign of her. He found none. "Hallo! Hallo!" he shouted, but only the tumult of the ship answered.

He stood there, pondering the fate of the girl. If she

had gone in blind terror into the social hall, she could not have survived.

Out of the six of them trapped below, only he and Kieley were still alive. But for how long? Filled with the urgency to get out of this trap, Moore again began to explore the possibilities of escape to the top deck.

There *had* to be a way out.

Looking at the wild seas rushing shoreward, Alex Ledingham knew that nothing could reach them from the shore, and nobody from the ship would make it *to* the shore. What to do, where to go, now? His eyes swept the devastation aft. He had no faith in the incongruous little shack squatting before the smokestack; the Marconi house had been "tacked on" to the deck when wireless became an important safety factor to ships at sea. It was not going to be standing for very long, in his opinion.

He turned his attention to the bow. It was well above water, and the seamen's quarters there were protected by the hull itself; if he could reach it he felt reasonably sure of survival.

Somebody was already there. A couple of times he had glimpsed the figure of a man waving to attract their attention, ducking back inside when the seas swept aboard. Could he reach it?

Beside him, Jacob Pinsent was also studying the bow. "What chance have we to make it to the fo'c's'le?" Ledingham shouted.

"I'm gonna try it," Pinsent shouted back.

"So will I," Ledingham said. He turned to Mate James and passenger James Miller close by: "We're going to try and get forward; watch what we do and follow us."

Pinsent maneuvered down over the wreckage,

dropped the last ten feet to the deck below, and sprinted to the forecastle. He reached it and Joseph Burry hauled him inside.

"Did you see George Crocker?" Burry asked anxiously.

Pinsent told him bluntly, "He was in the wheelhouse when I saw him last."

There was no time for speculation about Crocker's fate. The door had been wrenched off, and they had to hang on or be swept outside. Clinging to the door frame, they watched for other survivors who might be attempting the dangerous run across the deck.

Ledingham dropped to the deck just as the sea lifted over the side. It swept him amongst the winches where he grasped the derrick coils hanging in front of the mast. The sea battered him mercilessly, then dropped him on the winches, cutting his leg to the bone. Ledingham did not feel the injury; he had only moments before the next sea boarded. It caught him as he lifted his foot to enter the forecastle, and flung him into the bow, dropping him on the windlass as it hit the steel plates.

Ledingham had the wind knocked out of him briefly, but he recovered enough to wrap his arms around the windlass and hold on. When the sea receded, he scrambled to his feet and staggered to the little room. Pinsent and Burry pulled him inside, looked at the gashed and bleeding leg, assisted him into a bunk, and piled some sodden blankets around him.

Ledingham's watch had stopped at 7:45 A.M., the time of his first immersion. When he got to the forecastle, a battered old timepiece there was still ticking away. It was 8:00 A.M.

With his face gashed and bleeding, Philip Jackman scurried toward the smokestack, but noticing the partially open door of the Marconi house, he swerved and went inside. Quartermaster Thomas Green and William Molloy followed him.

When Dave Griffiths came to, he was in the little wireless room, but how he got there he would never know. His shins were badly scraped but he was unaware of it.

Captain Martin had survived the giant seas, though he was severely knocked about. He found himself hanging to the handrail around the Marconi house. Soon the sound of voices impressed itself upon his mind, and he hauled himself around to the entrance. He heard someone calling his name: "It's Captain Martin. Come in, sir."

It was some consolation to see that it was crammed with people. They were a sorry-looking lot, but they looked good to Martin.

James and Miller had not followed Ledingham and Pinsent to the forecastle; Miller had been swept overboard and James sprinted to the smokestack, heading for the iron rungs on the side of the fiddley casing. He made it, clinging to the top of the fiddley out of the reach of the sea.

The sky was a flinty gray. The angry ocean heaved landward, expending the force of a thousand miles of ocean in a madly magnificent spectacle of Neptune's wrath. The shore, as far as the eye could see in either direction, snarled back in its own white anger.

James noted that a dory had been launched from the beach. It stood upright, suspended for a moment by the violent convolutions of the sea, then it capsized and was hurled back upon the shore. That was that, he thought.

He looked northeastward and saw, a mile or so away, black Renews Rocks jutting starkly out of deep water.

Closer inshore, and northward by a couple of miles, bleak, forbidding Renews Island was barely visible. The rocks lay roughly a mile and a half offshore, almost in a direct line with the *Florizel's* stern; they must have barely scraped by it.

James shuddered. If they had hit those rocks, there would have been nobody left to tell the tale.

Noah Dauphinee, Michael Power, and Charles Snow were part of the group still hugging the precarious shelter of the cabin. "We'd better get out of here," Power yelled.

He and Dauphinee made a run for the smokestack. Power ducked inside the fiddley, but Dauphinee, seeing Mate James on top of the fiddley casing, decided he would seek shelter there. He grabbed a wire stay anchoring the smokestack and climbed upward. Suddenly, there in front of him was the gaping cowl of a large ventilator; it looked dry and comfortable, and without thinking twice about it, he grabbed for it. "Help me!" he shouted to James, who obligingly gave him a heft into the cowl. It was cold and drafty, but the seas could sweep the *Florizel* and they would not touch Dauphinee.

Power did not stay in the fiddley very long. There were a couple of Spanish firemen there, both on the verge of collapse. They were clad only in singlets and pants, and how they had survived in such a state of undress was beyond Power's understanding. He stuck his head outside to look for other survivors, and saw the bodies of more Spanish firemen, and the body of Charlie Snow washing about the deck. The Marconi house seemed to offer more comfortable quarters, and he made a dash for it.

Nor did Mate James stay long on the top of the fiddley casing. Cramped and cold, he eased down over the side and went inside. The two firemen were there, but in a few minutes, one collapsed and died. Only José Fernandez was left.

Noting a piece of tarpaulin in the corner of the fiddley, James picked it up and gave it to Fernandez, indicating that he should put it over his head to protect himself from the water dripping upon him.

Taking a look outside, he saw a man standing on the deck. He appeared to be in a daze until James pulled him inside the fiddley. It was Lieutenant Ralph Burnham.

Through salt-bleared eyes, John Cleary stared at what he thought was an apparition. Clinging to the handrail beside him in the lee of the captain's cabin was a slender young woman.* She was skimpily clad, with long black hair hanging below her waist. From what unlikely niche on the wreck had she come?

"Can you save me?" she implored.

There was only the dubious protection of the wrecked wall between them and death. In his Newfoundland Irish twang, Cleary replied, "Girl, I don't think I can even save meself."

They hugged the shelter, waiting for they knew not what. The young woman slid to the deck, sitting on the tattered remnant of a lifeboat cover that had been swept there. A giant wave rolled toward them, lifted her, carried her over the side. Cleary was engulfed, but when it passed he saw her, still sitting on the tarpaulin, with hair flying, riding to her death on the top of the wave as it thundered shoreward. The incredible sight burned on his brain, and he knew he had to find shelter or meet the same fate.

Only the smokestack seemed impervious to the de-

* Probably Annie Dalton.

structive force of the savage seas, and Cleary determined to make a run for it. Being a devout Roman Catholic, he made the sign of the cross over the seething deck, then rushed for the smokestack. He made it safely and hurtled into the fiddley. In a few minutes he was followed by his friend, Jack Sparrow. He did not know where Sparrow came from, but he was happy to see him.

"Did you see Andy or Paddy?" Sparrow asked.

"Paddy's lost," Cleary said.

Major Sullivan had watched men die around him; one by one they had given up the unequal struggle and let the seas take them; but his own bulldog determination to live permitted no such thought to enter his mind. Of all the survivors who had taken shelter forward, only two others hung doggedly to what was left of the captain's cabin. Each sea demolished it further, and to remain there was the height of folly. He bawled: "I think we'd better try and get to the smokestack."

Clambering over the steel lifeboat, he hurtled across the deck, but the sea caught him midway and carried him toward the mass of wreckage on the starboard side. He caught at a wire stay and held on until the sea went over. When it passed, he crawled to the Marconi house and pulled himself up by the handrail. It did not occur to him that there might be survivors inside; at this moment he did not know if there *were* any other survivors.

He went inside the fiddley and found Mate James, José Fernandez, Ralph Burnham, John Cleary, and Jack Sparrow. Looking back for his two companions, he saw one of them wash overboard; of the other there was no sign.

William Parmiter lay in the lee of the steel lifeboat jammed against the railing, secure for the moment but wondering if he was the only one alive. Looking toward the bow, he saw no sign of life and concluded that no one could possibly survive in that place. The aft view, with the seas falling over the smokestack and the Marconi house, was equally terrifying, but the smokestack looked as if it could offer good protection if he could reach it.

He decided he had no choice but to try.

Parmiter plotted his course. He could see the iron rungs on the side of the fiddley casing, and decided that if he could get there, he was as good as saved. Noting a stay between himself and the smokestack, he made a run for it and grabbed it just a wave engulfed him. When it passed, he sprinted to the fiddley casing, climbed quickly to the top, and hugged the shelter of the huge funnel. It was not very satisfactory. The sea did not touch him, but the biting wind froze his body, and the view below was downright disheartening. The men watching from the beach gave him no great hope either; it was obvious they could not help him for some time.

Huddled miserably against the smokestack, he thought he heard voices coming from the little house squatting on the deck below. Hurriedly he came off the fiddley top and ran for the door. It was warped and firmly stuck, but he forced it open and managed to squeeze inside.

There were no people dodging the seas now; only the dead floated with the surge and pull of the waves. Thirty-two survivors were jammed in the Marconi room, six were in the fiddley, three were in the forecastle, one was in the ventilator atop the fiddley, and two were trapped below.

PART IV

# Rescue

# CHAPTER 16

*ST. JOHN'S WAS* slowly awakening. Sleet raked the town, wisps of smoke were torn from chimney tops as the wind scoured rooftops and whistled around corners. Slush covered the streets, rivers of mud and snow flowed over the steep hills. The solid bulk of the Southside Hills sheltered the port from the great Atlantic combers, though they heaved in through The Narrows, creating a rough passageway for any ship daring to venture outside. Cape Spear was recording mountainous seas, and down the coast, Cape Race reported southwest winds blowing a gale.

In the shelter of the harbor, ships lay snugly at their moorings. Many were in various stages of readiness for the annual seal hunt, scheduled for mid-March; other ships were lying up with no steam, no crews aboard.

H.M.S. *Briton*, naval training ship for Newfoundland Reservists, was tied up at the naval wharf. Newfoundland seamen were trained aboard her for naval warfare before shipping overseas, but *Briton* seldom, if ever, moved from her anchorage, and was more or less a naval barracks. Present Commanding Officer was Captain Anthony MacDermott.*

* Acting Commander for the period of the war.

Only one ship, the whaler *Hawk*, had steam up and a busy crew, and she was preparing to sail northward to Harbour Grace with a load of coal. Scheduled time of sailing: 7:00 A.M.

The insistent ringing of the telephone disturbed the household of the Honourable John C. Crosbie,* Minister of Shipping, Minister of Finance and Customs, general merchant, shipowner, and brought that gentleman grumpily out of bed. It was, he noted, 5:15 A.M., an ungodly hour to be dragged out of bed on a Sunday. It had been a rotten night and it was still rotten, according to the weather beating against the house. Crosbie was one of the few hundred people who had a telephone in St. John's at the time; it would therefore be an important call.

He lifted the receiver and a crisp, British voice spoke in his ear. "Commander MacDermott here. Our men at the transmitting station in Mount Pearl says there's been an S.O.S. from the *Florizel* that she's going to pieces near Cape Race."

Crosbie was staggered. "What?" His good friend, John Munn, had sailed on the *Florizel*; aside from that, his mind did not run to shipwreck but rather to German enemy action, which he recalled had been responsible for the loss of the *Stephano* in 1916. "Has she been submarined?"

"I don't think so," MacDermott replied, "but that's all the information we have: she's ashore near Cape Race and fast going to pieces — that was the message."

Crosbie thought swiftly. Today was Sunday; they were going to have a problem finding a ship with a crew already aboard. On top of that, it would take hours to prepare a ship for rescue work. He told MacDermott, "You try and keep in touch with the *Florizel* and I'll get

* Later Sir John Crosbie.

in touch with Eric Bowring to find out if they have a ship ready to send up to her. I'll call you back."

"Right," MacDermott said.

Crosbie, a man of great physical and mental vitality, wasted no time. Rousing his household, he settled down to the telephone. But Eric Bowring did not answer his telephone; nor did the Honourable John Harvey of Harvey and Company, agents for Bowring's Red Cross Line; and after much precious time had passed, he called MacDermott. "I can't get through to anyone. Have you been in touch with the *Florizel* since?"

"No," MacDermott replied, "we've lost touch with her."

"Keep trying. *I'll* try and get through to Eric Bowring."

This time Bowring answered. He was quite agitated. "I've just had the news," he said. "What do you think, John — is it serious?"

Crosbie said bluntly, "The message said she was fast going to pieces. I think you'll have to get a ship there immediately. What about the *Terra Nova*?"

Bowring was uncertain. The *Terra Nova* was probably their oldest ship; she had taken Robert Scott to the Antarctic on his doomed expedition in 1910* and had acquitted herself well at the icefields each year, but she was old and very slow. Right now she was being prepared for the seal hunt. "I don't know if she's ready."

"I saw steam on her yesterday afternoon; she shouldn't take too long to fire up. I'll get after the marine superintendent to get a crew aboard as quickly as possible so they can get away."

Crosbie got quickly through to Matthew McGettigan, the marine superintendent, and told him the news. "Get everything moving, round up a crew and get up there," he ordered.

* Scott and his party died in the Antarctic in March, 1912.

Crosbie next contacted the Honourable Tasker Cook,* a member of the Newfoundland Legislative Council, and got a promise of assistance to organize the rescue operation. "Can you come up to the house?" Crosbie asked.

"I'll be with you in a few minutes," Cook said.

H. D. Reid was the next. The Reid Newfoundland Company officially provided railway and steamship transportation in and around Newfoundland. At the present time the *Home*, a passenger freighter, was in port. Reid answered the telephone only after a considerable time. Crosbie told him, "The *Florizel's* in trouble at Cape Race, Harry, Do you have a ship at the dock that's ready to steam up there?"

"What kind of trouble?" Reid asked.

"I don't know. MacDermott called to say there was an s.o.s. with the message that she was going to pieces near Cape Race. Can you get a ship up there?"

Reid replied, "I can't say for sure, but I think the *Home* could be made ready in a couple of hours. I'll get in touch with the dispatching office and tell them to alert the crew. I'll be in touch as soon as I find out how everything is going."

Crosbie was satisfied with this. Things were moving fairly swiftly.

It was now 6:30 A.M. and the weather was improving.

The whaler *Hawk*, owned by the Newfoundland Shipbuilding Company, had steam up and was ready to sail to Harbour Grace with a cargo of coal from Bowring's. The wind was dropping, the sky was clearing, but great combers were heaving in through The Narrows. Captain Marcus Simonsen made his way to the office of Bowring's southside premises to use the telephone. Be-

* Later Sir Tasker Cook.

fore venturing outside The Narrows, he would check with the lighthouse keeper at Cape St. Francis, some twenty miles north of St. John's, to find out how rough it was outside.

Bowring's man was upset. "The *Florizel's* on the rocks," he told Simonsen, and passed along the meager details.

"Is anyone lost?" Simonsen asked.

"We only know she's ashore and going to pieces."

That sounded ominous enough to Simonsen, who changed his mind about sailing to Harbour Grace. He telephoned the office there. "I'll stay here, they'll probably need us," he said.

He hurried back to the *Hawk* to make preparations and to await orders to proceed to the wrecked ship. He had no doubt that he would quickly receive such orders since he had steam up and was ready to sail.

Crosbie had barely hung up when MacDermott called again. "I haven't been able to contact the *Florizel*; she hasn't been transmitting since that first message."

"That sounds bad."

"We'll keep trying, but it doesn't look good."

"That's all you can do, keep trying. We have the *Terra Nova* and the *Home* so far — at least we think they're available; we've got to get every available ship in the harbor."

"We'll keep trying on this end," MacDermott said.

Crosbie made one more call. It was to the dispatching office of the Dominion Coal Company. Their ship, the *Cape Breton*, had arrived in port on Tuesday and her cargo of coal had already been discharged. She should be readily available.

She was not. "The *Cape Breton* is in the middle of the drydock, sir," the clerk informed him.

Undaunted, Crosbie rang the residence of McAlpine, Superintendent of Dominion Coal, and explained the situation. McAlpine was very cooperative. "I'll go to the dock immediately and see about getting her ready," he said.

The dock was a good mile away and McAlpine had to use horse and sleigh to get there quickly.

Harry Reid called next. "John, I think we can get the *Home* ready; all hands will be aboard shortly."

Now things were really moving.

It was a short time later that the Honourable Tasker Cook arrived, and Crosbie briefed him. "If all goes well we've got the *Terra Nova*, the *Home*, and the *Cape Breton*. It's imperative to get as many steamers as we can find, and send them to Cape Race as quickly as possible."

Cook said, "Then I'll get along to Bowring's dispatching office and get working at it immediately."

John Crosbie had a hasty breakfast, ordered his horse and sleigh, and drove to Bowring's residence. The Honourable John Harvey was there with Eric Bowring, who looked pale and strained. Eric was a nephew of Sir Edgar Bowring and a director of the firm. With Sir Edgar holidaying in Florida and John Munn aboard the wreck, Eric was next in command.

There had been no further news of the *Florizel*; all attempts to contact her had failed and it was not known exactly where she had run ashore. "We can only suppose the wireless apparatus is out of commission," Bowring said, adding, "I've been in consultation with our company's ships' husband,* Captain Abram Kean, and with Marine Superintendent McGettigan, and they're preparing the *Terra Nova* to proceed to the rescue. Joe Kean sailed on the *Florizel* yesterday. Captain Kean will get things moving."

* The supervising officer in a fleet of ships belonging to a company.

Prominent and controversial, Captain Abram Kean had the reputation of doing the seemingly impossible. Joe Kean was his son and he would not rest until he had a ship under way.

The telephone rang and Eric Bowring answered. He listened silently to the voice on the other end, then slowly replaced the receiver. "It's Cappahayden. She's ashore at Cappahayden, and she's going to pieces."

"Cappahayden?"

They were mystified. If the *Florizel* had run ashore at Cappahayden, she must have been wrecked hours earlier — but why hadn't she sent out a call for help when she struck? Surely it hadn't taken her until 5:00 A.M. to reach Cappahayden.

The news spread but was garbled. Mariners, estimating the average speed of steamers going along the coast, figured the *Florizel* had gone ashore somewhere around 1:00 A.M. She had not sent out a distress call earlier, and it was assumed her crew and passengers had made it safely ashore.

Mary Jackman had arisen early and was preparing to go to seven o'clock Mass. For some reason the lonely, plaintive sound of the *Florizel's* whistle had stayed with her throughout the night, keeping her on the edge of sleep.

Below, in the hallway, she heard the murmur of voices as Mrs. Drover conversed with a neighbor who had dropped in, ". . . it's terrible," she heard.

"What's terrible?" she called from the stairway.

There was a startled pause, then Mrs. Drover called back, "The streets are in a terrible state, Mary; you'd better put on long rubbers when you go to church."

They went into the kitchen and closed the door while Mary looked out of her bedroom window. It was a gray morning, the streets were slushy, but not *that* slushy. Vaguely uneasy, she finished dressing and hurried downstairs to the kitchen to find Mrs. Drover and her friend whispering together. They stopped guiltily. *Something was up!*

She said, "What's happened?"

They looked unhappy.

"Is it the *Florizel*?" Mary asked.

Mrs. Drover burst out, "She went ashore last night," then, as Mary changed color and looked ready to faint, she added, "but they've all landed at Renews. They're all saved."

Her breath and her color came back, but her heart was racing furiously. "Praise be to God," she murmured.

She was not a woman to go to pieces, and she set about planning dinner. "Phil will want his dinner when he comes," she said.

She did not question the story, nor let any other thought crowd in on her. She had been told that Phil was safe, and that was good enough for her. She would go to a later Mass and offer up prayers of gratitude that her Phil was alive and safe, but right now she would prepare his dinner.

Dora Crocker had no premonition of disaster when she arose. She fed the baby and prepared breakfast, but her attention was drawn to the astonishing number of people passing by the house. In spite of the unpleasant weather, everybody in town must have gone to church this morning, she thought.

She peered out the front window and decided that something was up; men and women were standing in groups, gesticulating and talking excitedly.

She had to know what was going on.

She called the girls: "Get up, all of you, something's going on and I'm going down the street to find out what it's all about."

Putting on her coat and hat, Dora Crocker went outside and walked to the first group of people. A man turned to her and said: "Terrible news this mornin', Missus, the *Florizel's* gone down; all hands are lost."

Reeling with shock, Dora made it back to her house. She could not really absorb what the man had said; she had to get back to her family.

Baby Clem was fussing.

Mary Maloney eased out of bed, hurried clumsily into her clothes, and picked him up. Young Albert was rattling the lids of the stove as he lit the fire in the kitchen; the children were already awake and getting noisier by the minute. Would she find the energy, this day, to get meals for seven hungry children?

She had not slept well. Had not, in fact, slept at all after "The Light" had wakened her.

Remembering, she shuddered. Had it been a dream?

Midway between sleep and wakefulness last night, she had become aware of a light. It appeared to be the golden light of a single candle, which grew steadily bigger, brighter, and all-pervading, searing her brain with the intensity of its brightness, unaccountably terrifying her to full consciousness. Heart thudding against her ribs, breath strangling in her throat, she had struggled upright in bed. *Something had happened to Greg!*

The southeast wind sweeping into the bay had moaned around the house, rattled the windowpanes, adding to the terror welling up inside her. Besieged by the most fearsome thoughts, she had spent the remainder of the night trying to push them aside, but the intensity of the dream — if it had been a dream — had kept her twisting and turning, too frightened to close her eyes. Something had happened to Greg, she was positive of that.

She looked out into the gray morning. Sish ice had packed into the bay and piled up on the shore; steep waves, controlled by the ice, rolled on the land. It did not look wild, but she recognized the fury of the icebound waves.

She went heavily downstairs. Whatever had happened, she had the children to think of.

# 17

IT WAS broad daylight now. The *Florizel* jolted and bounced as the seas rolled over and spilled upon the Marconi house; the roof was beginning to split under the strain, and the sea dripped coldly upon the survivors. The resounding boom of the sea was a ceaseless din that stretched the nerve ends and left them in fear and expectation of death.

The wind had gone around to the east-northeast and was dropping, but the ship was icing up. The survivors, although packed tightly together, derived little if any heat from one another. Although Minnie and Kitty had blankets around their heads and shoulders, their bodies were totally without feeling.

Johnston had kept a protective eye on Minnie, continually adjusting the blanket around her. "You're all right, Miss Denief," he reassured her.

Carter had taken Kitty under his wing and kept straightening her blanket each time it went awry.

Philip Jackman was in agony with his dislocated shoulder and the salt water dripping on his bloodied, broken face. His nose was almost completely lopped off, leaving an exposed, shattered nose bone; his teeth were smashed, his left cheek was laid open and caked with blood. Someone ripped a steward's jacket apart and wound it around his face; Johnston had found another blanket and wrapped it around his head and shoulders.

Jackman bore it all silently.

Captain Martin, recovered somewhat, roused himself enough to think of rescue operations. His career, his reputation, were as wrecked as the *Florizel*, but he still had a responsibility to the survivors.

He stepped outside. It was evident that the Marconi house and its occupants were precariously situated. Earlier, from the bridge, he had noted that the sea lost some of its momentum after it hit the smokestack and therefore fell upon the little house with less devastating power. They were alive only because the smokestack took the brunt of the waves; even so, if the roof splintered, the Marconi house would twist and buckle as the wheelhouse had and they would all perish. He *had* to do *something*.

He saw the people of Cappahayden were still standing helplessly on the beach about 200 yards away.

Seaman Dooley had followed him outside, and Martin said to him, "We must get a line ashore somehow and rig a breeches buoy."

The suggestion was sheer folly, but Dooley replied, "I'll help you, Cap'n."

Then, over the tumult of ship and ocean, they heard voices coming from the direction of the smokestack. "Someone's in the fiddley!" Dooley cried.

They dashed over there and looked upon a ludicrous sight. A handful of men, one of them Major Sullivan, were bunched under a small tarpaulin; they were clustered around a dark-skinned Spanish fireman, rubbing and pounding his body and *breathing* on him. "We're trying to keep him warm," Sullivan said.

Martin's spirits lifted a little at finding more survivors. More than ever, it was imperative to get a line ashore so these lives could be saved before the ship disintegrated completely. A desperate plan was forming in his mind. "There's no hope in the world of the men on shore getting a line aboard of us," he said to Mate James, "but I could tie a line around myself and swim ashore."

Sullivan was incredulous. "In *that* sea?"

While Martin had no wish to die, he felt he had little alternative but to follow this plan through. "There's no other way," he said.

"You'll drown!"

Martin was aware of that probability and said so. "At least they'll get my body with the line attached, and that's what counts," he said flatly.

"There are no lines, Captain; everything is washed away," Mate James said.

"There's bound to be some lines in the fo'c's'le," Martin stated. "I'll have to try and get forward as soon as the seas go down a little."

Being a master mariner himself, Mate James did not argue with the captain, but he did not like the idea at all.

Martin and Dooley stayed there awhile, Martin staring glumly at the great combers rushing past. Wreckage not caught in the starboard rail was gradually sweeping away. Bodies washed back and forth. The rigging, the mast, the railings that remained were growing a crust of ice; the deck was treacherously slippery.

Nothing could be done for the time being, but Martin kept slipping in and out of the Marconi room as if hoping for some miraculous change in their situation. The split in the roof kept widening and the ship lurched about, shifting a little as she pounded over the rocks. Someone muttered that the *Florizel* could not stand too much more and she would soon break in half. There was truth in that. The stern had been straining to break away ever since she struck and it could happen any time.

Minnie asked Johnston, "What will happen if the Marconi room breaks in half?"

He joked, "Why, you go one way and I go the other." He added, "But I don't think it will break in half, Miss Denief."

In Minnie's eyes particularly, Johnston was a hero. He was more so now as he kept up a stream of jokes and light banter, massaging the numbed survivors close to him, patting their faces to stimulate circulation, and generally keeping up their spirits. "You'll be all right, ol' man," he encouraged a shivering steward. Maloney was the only one who did not respond.

The sea dripped continuously on Dave Griffiths' head, and as the split widened, he became nearly insensible with the cold. It was Johnston who grabbed a pillow from the bunk drawer and stuffed it up into the gap. "That'll keep the water off you," he said cheerfully. From that moment on, Dave began to collect his senses.

The hours crawled by, but the seas did not moderate in spite of a clearing day, and there was still no rescue ship in sight. Captain Martin was continually searching the horizon for smoke. Like all seamen who had been on duty when the ship struck, he was fully dressed.

From the fiddley opening Mate James also kept a watch to seaward, expecting to see the smoke of several ships approaching. Sullivan grumbled, "Surely if the s.o.s. had been picked up they would have been here long ago."

James had to agree. "Even if the s.o.s. wasn't picked up, the land telegraph station here in Cappahayden would have sent the alarm hours ago."

"Then where is everybody?" Cleary asked.

The storm had dumped four to five inches of snow over west Newfoundland, and the center had stalled over the Deer Lake area, where it began to dissipate. On the southeast coast the wind began to drop and veer southward, causing a heavy, confused sea in the Cape Race area. There was little change inside the Bantems where the *Florizel* lay.

With stoic calm the survivors in the Marconi room waited for rescue. A few prayed for them all.

Then it happened. With the nerve-wracking screech of tearing metal, the stern section broke away, and the *Florizel* bounced up and down and swung from side to side in a frightening manner as the seas rushed over and through her. She banged and scraped on the rocks with such violence that the survivors in the Marconi room cried out in terror.

"She's going, men, she's finished!"

"God help us!"

"Merciful Lord help us . . . "

"We'll all drown now!"

"She's sinking!"

Over the din, Captain Martin spoke with authority. "It's all right, only the stern has fallen off. She'll swing back and forth a bit more, but *she can't sink*."

The *Florizel* could not sink, but she was considerably lightened; her cargo would float from number three hold, lightening her further so that the hull would beat about, perhaps shift. And if she did shift her position, the sea could easily smash the Marconi house. Martin felt that he had no alternative now but to find a rope and swim to shore.

He took off his jacket and passed it to Lumsden, but replaced his lifebelt; then he removed his boots.

Bewildered, Lumsden asked, "What are you doing, Cap'n?"

He replied, "I'm going to try and swim ashore. Who has no boots?"

A pair of eager hands reached for them.

"I'll go with you, Cap'n." Dooley also took off his jacket and boots and passed them to Fred Roberts.

Lumsden protested, "But Cap'n, it's madness, you'll never survive."

"I'm a strong swimmer."

There were murmurs of protest from the crowd. "Don't do it, sir."

Martin was firm, "I will tie a rope around me, if I don't make it" — he gestured — "they'll get my body and they'll have a line to the ship; you can rig a breeches buoy then."

"You can't do it, sir."

"It's our only chance as far as I can see."

Lumsden accepted this decision unwillingly. "If you think you can make it, you can only try, but you're mad to even think of it," he said bluntly. "Anyway, there are no lines; everything is swept away."

"I'm sure there will be some lines in the rooms under the fo'c's'le head — there's all kinds of stuff there. I'm bound to find something."

A survivor squirmed out of his lifebelt and handed it to Dooley, "You'll need it," he said.

Fully prepared to swim ashore, both men left the Marconi house, taking with them the good wishes of the survivors. With no boots and without the protection of their heavy jackets, their bodies quickly numbed as they waited for that brief interval between seas to get forward. How they made the drop to the deck, ten feet below, was a feat neither remembered too clearly. In the forecastle they found an astonished Jacob Pinsent and Joseph Burry crouching in their little room. Alex Ledingham was lying in the bunk, his leg gashed and swollen.

"It's the Cap'n and Dooley!" Pinsent and Burry were deeply moved by the sight of the two dripping, weary men. "We thought, sir, we was the only ones left."

"There's more back in the Marconi house and the fiddley, between thirty and forty, I should say," Martin told them.

Burry asked, "Did George Crocker get saved?"

"No," Dooley told him, "he went overboard with the wheelhouse."

Martin and Dooley began to search the tiny rooms for lines. There was nothing. The carpenter's shop and the little cubbyhole with the odds and ends of stuff had been swept clean.

"I need lines. Where will I find them?" Martin demanded. Now that his mind was made up, he felt the urge to get on with the swim to shore.

"Everything is gone, Cap'n. There's some lines outside under the water in the bow, but we can't get at 'em," Pinsent said.

Ledingham asked, "What do you want with lines, Captain Martin?"

"I'm going to take a line ashore," Martin told him.

Wincing with pain, Ledingham sat up. "What good is that going to do?" he reasoned. "Nothing can be done for us until the sea goes down. Even if your body does drift ashore, what can they do? I ask you, what can they do? *Nothing!*"

There was silence as Ledingham's eyes bored fiercely into Martin's. Dooley, Pinsent, and Burry were like graven images.

Martin spoke quietly, hopelessly: "You know I'm going to be crucified over this."

Ledingham snorted. "So you'll be crucified, so you'll be a nine-day wonder. Is that any reason to throw your life away? You've got a wife and children in St. John's, what's going to happen to them?"

"I hadn't thought about it," Martin confessed.

"Well, think about it. This'll blow over, man, the same as everything else."

Martin groaned. "But Mr. Munn is lost, and his little girl . . ."

"There's no question that it'll be rough on you," Ledingham told him, "but it will blow over. Everything blows over eventually."

"Perhaps," Martin said. He did not feel that it would blow over. He turned to Dooley. "At the turn of the tide the seas won't be so heavy, we'll swim ashore then."

Ledingham said vehemently, "It's madness!"

"No," Martin said, "the seas will smooth out at the turn of the tide and we should have no real hardship to get ashore."

Swimming through stormy seas in mid-winter was not desirable, but it was not an impossible feat either. Half a century before, Captain William Jackman had swum the same distance to a wrecked ship in raging seas not once but twenty-seven times. It had been a superhuman feat, but it had been done.

Meanwhile, there could be no question of getting back up over the superstructure to the Marconi house. He and Dooley would wait in the forecastle and try for the ropes at the first opportunity. He took a look at Ledingham's injured leg. "Nasty," he said, and removing the boot, rubbed Ledingham's foot to restore circulation.

The seas surged in and out of the little room and Martin took a couple of sodden blankets from another berth, tacked them over the opening. It didn't help. The seas swept under and through the flimsy bedding.

Joseph Moore had just about given up hope of finding a way out of his watery prison. The continuous noise of the grating hull, the inner turmoil of the ship, made it difficult for him to think clearly.

There had been some frightful banging around and the seas had gone mad when the stern had broken off, but it had not noticeably worsened his situation. More light filtered through the submerged alleyway aft, but it revealed, once and for all, that there was no place for him to go.

Moore waded into the cross-alleyway, feeling as though he had been buried alive, and fear was growing that it might well become his tomb. The man and the boy lay dead and frozen in Room 19; Miss Keough was frozen in a kneeling position in the upper berth in Kieley's room, and Kieley himself had been unusually quiet in the closet.

*He had to get out.*

For the first time he opened the door of the linen closet in the cross-alleyway. It was a fairly spacious walk-in closet, comparatively dry and quite bright. Moore's heart raced with excitement. A partition separated the linen closet from the skylight shaft that extended to the pantry on the deck below, and it did not go right to the ceiling; the top of the partition had been made of glass to let the daylight into the linen closet. The glass had shattered and the water flooding through the skylight sent sprays into the closet. Great steam pipes curved around the ceiling and disappeared into the walls.

Moore clambered up over the closet shelves to the open partition and stuck his head into the pantry shaft. A shiver ran up his spine. The shaft was filled with black sea water, licking and sucking at the paneling as it surged through the ship. Moore contemplated his position. The skylight combing was just beyond his reach. He was tall and lean and had very long arms and legs.

Could he project himself outward into the shaft and upward to the combing at the same time? He took one more look into the deep shaft at the seas reaching hungrily upward. Well, he thought, if he didn't make it, that was all there was to it. Pray to God he would.

He propelled himself upward; his long, sinewy arms shot out and reached for the edge of the skylight . . .

His hands closed over the combing, and, with the strength born of desperation, he hoisted his body up. Then he was through the skylight.

Moore had no time to take in the terrible devastation. He was immediately beside the fiddley casing and he saw the door of the Marconi house partially open. He ran toward it. The door was jammed and resisted him, but hearing voices inside, he shouted, "Let me in!"

A voice shouted back, "There's no room in here, we're jammed tight."

Frantically, Moore dashed back to the smokestack, spied the fiddley opening, and rushed inside. He could have wept with joy at the sight of the handful of men there, clustering around the Spaniard, rubbing briskly to keep him alive.

"Did you come from the Marconi room?" Mate James asked.

"From below," Moore replied. "I got up through the skylight. Mr. Kieley is still down there in his room."

"We can't help him *yet*," James said.

Moore told them of the situation below and Sullivan mourned, "I have three bottles of whisky in my room, if I could only get at it, it would warm our insides."

Cleary said fervently, "Don't I wish you could." Although he wore only singlet and pants, he did not feel the cold.

Still in the closet in Room 2, John Kieley slept soundly.

CHAPTER 18

THE PORT of St. John's buzzed with the news of the wrecked *Florizel*. Messages were flowing in from the Cappahayden Telegraph Office and the public learned the worst: she was indeed going to pieces and bodies were washing ashore.

In the quarantine hospital, Chief Officer John Tucker was shaken but puzzled when he heard the news. "Cappahayden! If she's ashore at Cappahayden, she must've grounded about half past one," he stated.

That was the impression in marine circles, and why she had not sent out an s.o.s. until 5:00 A.M. was a mystery.

Most of the passengers and crew were residents of St. John's, and thousands jammed Water Street, moving between the Anglo Telegraph office and Bowring's own cable office. The authorities were busy setting the rescue in motion, but a strange thing was happening: *everybody was so furiously organizing, nothing was actually getting started.*

The *Hawk*, ready to sail since 7:00 A.M., was still in port at eight o'clock; no orders had come to Captain Simonsen to proceed to the wreck and he did not have the authority to do so while in port. When informed of the wreck in the early hours, Cyril W. Tessier, agent for the *Hawk*, had given his chief assistant orders to contact Simonsen, "He's to get ready and go up to Cape Race." Then he ordered the first delaying message, "Tell him I'm on my way to the dock and to meet me there."

Before Tessier left his house, a Bowring's official telephoned. "Foley here. You've heard about the *Florizel*?"

Tessier said he had.

"The *Hawk* is in the harbor, isn't she?"

"She is, and I've already sent word to Captain Simonsen to get ready to proceed immediately to the scene of the disaster. I'm going to the dock now."

"I'll join you there." Foley rang off.

It was nine o'clock before Tessier and Foley arrived to find Simonsen impatient and ready to sail. He had borrowed an extra engineer and a fireman from another ship that was laid up, because, he had reasoned, it was still rough outside and if they had to stand by the *Florizel* all night, they would need an extra engineer and fireman. He told Tessier, "We're ready to shove off."

Tessier asked what equipment was aboard to help the survivors.

Simonsen showed him what he had, but Tessier and Foley said it was not enough. They would need more lines, ropes, rockets, flashlights, acetylene lamps, and even another dory to supplement their own two dories. Foley suggested they drive back around the harbor to Bowring's retail store on Water Street to get the necessary equipment. Tessier agreed.

Simonsen seethed with impatience, but the *Hawk* was further delayed.

Learning of the disaster, Captain Ernest Perry of the *Gordon C*, owned by P. H. Cowan and Company, had steam up by eight o'clock and was standing by, expecting orders to sail every moment.

By nine o'clock, however, orders still had not come.

The *Home*, as promised by H. D. Reid, had steam up and could have sailed by eight o'clock, but she was still waiting for a crew.

The *Cape Breton* was not available, McAlphine regretfully informed the Honourable John Crosbie; her fires were low, she was empty and had no ballast and would be quite unmanageable in the heavy seas pounding the coast.

Crosbie, in company with Eric Bowring, arrived at Bowring's cable office, now operating in full swing and sending a flood of questions to the Cappahayden operator. These messages to and from Cappahayden had to be relayed through the powerful Cape Race station and took a considerable period of time.

Captain Nicholas Kennedy and Marine Superintendent McGettigan were waiting there, and the news was not good. "We don't have a full crew for the *Terra Nova*," Kennedy announced.

That was the problem. It was Sunday and the crews of ships not scheduled to sail were scattered far and wide.

Crosbie thought the matter over. "I'm sure we can settle that easily enough. There are naval reservists on the *Briton*; I believe Commander MacDermott will let us have the number we want to crew the ships."

Contacted, MacDermott promised them any number of seamen: "They'll be there as soon as you need them."

It was going too slowly to suit Crosbie, and he asked Eric Bowring, "Where is the *Prospero*?"

The *Prospero** was another of Bowring's ships under

---

* Services around Newfoundland were expanding so swiftly that the Reid Newfoundland Company were unable to handle the traffic alone.

contract to the Newfoundland Government to carry mail and passengers around the island of Newfoundland. Bowring replied, "She's somewhere in Placentia Bay, on her way to Marystown."

That would put her roughly a hundred miles from the scene of the wreck.

"I think," Crosbie said, "we should telegraph Marystown and have them send her back to Cappahayden as soon as she arrives. She'll probably get there quicker than any other ship."

The *Prospero* was equipped with wireless, but because of war regulations, use of it was restricted, although she had a full-time operator on duty. It meant that precious time would be lost as she steamed on to Marystown.

The message was dispatched.

Having made arrangements with Commander Mac-Dermott for naval reservists to crew the rescue ships, Crosbie, Bowring, and Tasker Cook, who had assisted in the operations, discussed the possibility of sending a special train with doctors, nurses, and rescue equipment to Renews, the nearest railway station to Cappahayden, six miles away. "I'll call Harry Reid and see what he thinks about the idea," Crosbie said.

Reid thought it an excellent suggestion; it would take two to three hours to get a train ready, but he would get at it right away.

It was not until 9:50 A.M. that the Honourable John G. Stone, Minister of Marine and Fisheries, received notification of the wreck from the government wireless station at Cape Race:

> *Advise quickly if you are sending local assistance to Florizel, nearest ship at present is sixteen hours steaming from here, wish to conserve this ship's*

*coal and not turn her from course if quicker assistance is sent. Rush reply.*

J. Kerton,
*Officer in Charge.*

Learning of the disaster in greater detail, Stone tracked down John Crosbie and Eric Bowring at the railway station, and was informed of the progress of rescue operations up to that time. Assured that all was going smoothly, he returned to his office and sent word to Cape Race that local assistance was being rushed to the scene of the wreck. Then he headed for the railway station to see if he could be of further assistance.

Much was going on. As the special train was being made up, Doctors Cluny Macpherson* and Tom Anderson and several nurses arrived with all sorts of medical supplies. Stone's deputy minister, A. P. Goodridge, had brought a special rocket apparatus that could be used to shoot a lifeline aboard the wreck.

"All we need is someone to operate it," Stone observed.

"We'll get MacDermott to send a gunner," Crosbie said.

Soon Gunner Marshall arrived from the *Briton* and took over the apparatus.

Charles Steer, of Steers Limited, appeared at the railway and offered the services of the *Gordon C.* "She's at the wharf and ready to go," he told them.

The Minister of Marine and Fisheries said, "The *Hawk* is also ready to go."

"Dispatch everything you can get," Eric Bowring ordered.

Still no ships left the harbor.

* Inventor of the gas mask.

In church, Mary Jackman learned the truth: the *Florizel* was breaking up on the rocks at Cappahayden and Phil was still aboard. Mary shut her mind to all the wild probabilities, seeing only Phil's face before her eyes. She could not — would not — even consider the possibility of his being lost.

When she left the church, she went straight to the home of Captain Martin, where his wife Clara, a stout woman of middle years, was rocking with grief. The tears flowed readily when she saw Mary. She, too, had been prey to the most horrendous stories. "Mary," she wept, "there's not one of them saved."

Mary said stiffly, "Who told you that."

"They're gone! All dead!" Mrs. Martin burst into a paroxysm of grief. "Bill is gone. Oh Bill."

Mary could not stand it. She must not let her emotions run away with her. She would go home and wait for Phil.

Dora Crocker was beside herself. A great pall of doom, so intense it was almost physical, enveloped her. With great effort she tried to repudiate it, alternating between the black depths of despair and a fierce rejection of the probability of George's death. "He's safe, I *know* he is," she said. Then, in the depths again, she wanted to throw herself into the harbor, only steps away.

Amy had little time to think of Joe or her father. As the bad news from Cappahayden was posted outside the cable office, Dora plunged into deep depression, and Amy was greatly concerned for her. "Mother, you mustn't give in like that. Nobody knows who's lost or saved."

She had no certain feelings about her father, but she was absolutely confident that Joe was safe.

Mary Maloney had gradually pushed the dream into the

188

background. With seven children to feed and clean up after, there was little time to think about "The Light," which seemed less terrifying in the cosy warmth and clatter of the kitchen. The older boys had gone outdoors after breakfast, giving her more room to breathe and work.

The boys had barely gone, it seemed, when the door burst open and Albert rushed in. "Mom, the *Florizel's* ashore!" he yelled, voice shrill with shock and fright. "The telegraph office says she's ashore at Cappahayden, and they found Joe Kean's body on the beach!"

She couldn't speak.

The *Terra Nova* was ready to sail. Dr. J. G. Knowlton, the American, had volunteered his services, but they were still waiting for the naval reservists promised by Commander MacDermott. It was going too slowly for Abram Kean, and he had decided to go not on the old *Terra Nova* but with the rescue team on the special train. With such bad news bombarding them, he was most anxious about his son, and the train would get him to the wreck more quickly.

Kean's usually ruddy complexion was pale, his short, stocky figure was commanding in its stillness, the set face revealed nothing as he waited for the train to depart. In truth, Abram Kean was devastated. If he was known as an aloof and demanding captain on the bridge, his one vulnerable point was love of his sons. He was a strong family man, a patriarch who still ruled his family, but he loved them dearly.

The rescue train was almost ready, hissing and chuffing as last-minute emergency supplies were packed aboard. The doctors and nurses carried overnight bags. The Honourable Tasker Cook had been put in charge of the train, and he, too, was prepared for an overnight stay at the scene of the disaster. Bowring's had put one of their own wireless operators aboard; he would be right on the scene of the wreck and would "cut in" on the commercial land line to send information directly to Bowring's own cable office.

Suddenly a clerk from the railway dispatching office rushed out with a message which he passed to Eric Bowring. Bowring, visibly shocked when he read it, passed it to Abram Kean. It stated, baldly, that Captain Joe Kean's body had been washed ashore.

Abram Kean read it and his armor cracked. He wept unashamedly. Joe, his quiet, unassuming son, was drowned.

All were moved by Captain Kean's grief. They knew Joe Kean and admired him; Bowring had a deep affection for him. "We'll have to get Captain Kean home," he said.

Abram Kean allowed himself to be driven home and the relief train pulled out of the station half an hour later.

By the time Crosbie and Bowring arrived back at the Bowring premises, another message had arrived stating that the body* washed ashore was *not* that of Joe Kean. Bowring suggested, "Let's go to Captain Kean's house and tell him the good news," adding, "good news never hurt anybody."

Abram Kean received the message with great joy, but the relief train was gone and he wanted more than ever to get to Cappahayden.

It was Crosbie who provided the means: "The *Hawk* is going to Cappahayden; would you go in command of her?"

Abram Kean agreed, "I will, and I'll take my son, Westbury. He is here with me." Westbury had come

* It was the body of Second Officer John King.

from his own home to comfort his parents in their grief.

"Excellent," Bowring said. "It will save time if you collect the necessary clothing and equipment you may need from the store."

Bowring's general store was as busy as ever. It was here that they came upon Tessier and Simonsen. Crosbie told Simonsen, "Captain Kean is going up to the *Florizel* with you; he's practically in charge, and you will give him every assistance possible."

It was an order and, whatever his feelings, Simonsen nodded agreement.

Crosbie continued, "Captain Kean, you had better go with Simonsen and bring the *Hawk* over to this side, she's too deep in the water and they'll have to take some coal out of her."

Looking at the whaler across the harbor, Abram Kean muttered, "Yes, she's too deep in the water to get close to shore."

Simonsen, more impatient than ever to get moving, stated that they could throw the coal over the side as they were going up to Cape Race if need be.

But the order stood.

The *Hawk* was brought across the harbor and a large gang of men began to remove the coal with buckets while Simonsen and Tessier supervised the stowing of gear and provisions. Two volunteers, Captain Martin Dalton and Charles Pope, arrived to offer their services, and Tessier telephoned Commander MacDermott for some naval reservists to round out the crew.

Meanwhile the *Home* was still waiting for naval reservists. The Honourable John Stone was aboard, having decided that he would take a first-hand look at the situation.

It was 11:30 A.M. when the *Gordon C*, ready to steam since nine-thirty, finally received orders to go. She backed away from the wharf and steamed up the harbor, the first ship to slip through the red tape of the rescue operations.

The *Terra Nova*, with orders from Bowring's to remain at the scene of the wreck until all bodies had been recovered, followed close on the heels of the *Gordon C* with eight naval volunteers; and finally, at 12:45 P.M., the *Home* steamed out through The Narrows, with eight volunteers from the *Briton* rounding out her crew, Samuel Cooper and Walter Reid among them.

The news from Cappahayden was terribly discouraging. The stern had sunk, the seas were sweeping her, only the smokestack and the Marconi house were standing. Eric Bowring went home to grieve in private.

At 12:30 P.M. the *Hawk* was still discharging coal at Bowring's wharf, Abram Kean was inside the wharf premises with John Crosbie. The captain was restless and keyed up; time was hanging heavily when he so desperately wanted to be where he could help his son.

Crosbie said, "Go home and get your dinner, Captain Kean, by the time you're back, she'll be ready."

At that moment a clerk rushed in and passed a message to Crosbie. It read:

> The seas are washing all over the Florizel, all lives
> are lost, she is a total wreck.

*All lives lost!* In spite of the dreadful news coming over the wires, there had been hope that it was really not as bad as it sounded, but now . . .

He handed Captain Kean the cable.

Gray-faced, Abram Kean folded the cablegram and muttered, "It's all finished." He stared blindly ahead, his lips moving almost soundlessly. "Joe is dead, they're all dead. There's no use my going up there."

Equally devastated, Crosbie accepted the captain's decision. "I suppose if you think that way, there's no use."

Abram Kean muttered, "I must find Westbury and go home."

"I'll take you," Crosbie offered, and guided the old man from the wharf to the store. They found Westbury fitting himself with a suit of oilskins, and as father and son consoled each other, Crosbie found Tessier and told him about the message. "Tell the men to stop discharging coals, tell them to stop everything," he said.

Tessier said slowly, "Is it as bad as all that?"

"That's what the message said, they're all lost. It's too late to help them now."

Orders for the naval reservists were canceled, the coal bucket brigade stopped work, rescue equipment was piled back on the wharf. John Crosbie drove Abram and Westbury Kean to the captain's house, then he dropped in on the Bowring residence to pass Eric Bowring the grim news. Crosbie himself then returned to his own home, all of the vitality that had carried him through the morning now gone.

Aboard the *Hawk*, Tessier and Simonsen consulted. "What do you think?" Tessier asked.

Simonsen thought that in spite of the message some survivors might be on the wreck. "I think we should go up there anyway. I know the coast like I know the palm of my hand, the *Hawk* is ready enough, all we need is a crew. If we can get the Navy men we can leave now."

Tessier was more cautious. "I'll send a message to Cappahayden first," he said.

Another hour was lost before he received a reply from Cappahayden. The reply read:

> *Florizel position bad, under water aft; water going over her; spars and funnel standing; five men appeared on deck; assistance needed, no chance of rescuing them from land.*

Tessier returned posthaste to the *Hawk*. He had made the decision that their own company would send the ship. "There's life on the *Florizel* yet," he told Simonsen. "Get ready to sail, get the men back on the coal, and I'll get in touch with Mr. Crosbie and Mr. Bowring and Commander MacDermott."

Men were recalled, the rescue equipment, which had been removed, was stowed aboard, a few more tons of coal had to be removed and the men set to with a will. Tessier, meanwhile, telephoned Eric Bowring: "We cabled Cappahayden, and there's life aboard, but they can't be rescued from shore. The *Hawk* is going to the *Florizel* and we're sending her ourselves, if that's satisfactory," he said.

Bowring replied, "It is. Send her as quickly as possible."

More time was lost as Tessier sent a horse and sleigh to Captain Kean's home to ask if he still wanted to command the *Hawk*, but Abram Kean did not. He had little hope that his son was alive, his wife was in a state of shock, he himself was shattered.

When all was ready, they waited another hour before reservists Daniel J. Ralph, Michael Whelan, Michael Woodford, and Stephen Nash arrived, but at long last the *Hawk* was ready to sail. Just as she was about to slip her ropes, shouts went up from the crew: *Stowaways!* Two youngsters were put ashore and at 3:44 P.M. she was steaming up the harbor.

As if the red tape was not enough, the progress of the rescue ships was to be further hampered by heavy sish ice which, after pressing steadily on the land since the night before, had packed to a depth of three to four feet, and slowed the ships' speed by half.

# CHAPTER 19

*THE WEATHER* had cleared, and the wind was blowing briskly from the westward, flattening the seas offshore; but close to shore great combers still swept the *Florizel*. She was considerably lighter now, a dead ship. Most of her cargo of fish had floated free and had been flung upon the shore or was bobbing merrily northward, an indication that the Polar Current close to shore was not flowing on its usual southwesterly course. The forepart of the boat deck began to sag and split; gradually it was beaten down by the heavy seas and finally the ceiling of the social hall gave way and the deck caved in.

The survivors crushed together in the Marconi room gasped as one when it seemed that the structure would shake right off the deck. The portholes still held, although the two on the port side, taking the brunt of the seas, had cracked. Dave Griffiths was sure they were going to die; to him it felt as if they had all been jammed in a barrel and tossed into the wild ocean. The little house could not possibly take much more punishment, he thought. They would presently spill upon the black ugly rocks and die.

The fishermen of Cappahayden watched helplessly throughout the day. They had remained on the beach with their dories ready for launching at the first sign of moderating seas. They had lit a few fires and pulled bodies from the surf, but that was the extent of the help they had been able to give.

Men from the surrounding communities had been arriving all day. From Renews, fishermen had come, hauling their dories on long carts over the bleak, windswept hills. The snow had disappeared under the driving rain and the steep hills had made it a difficult task. First they would help in the rescue operations, then they would methodically strip the wreck of all salvageable parts. When they finished, there would be nothing worth taking on the *Florizel*.

They waited.

Below deck, John Kieley awoke, frozen, cramped, and sober to find the clothing on the lower part of his body encased in ice. He flexed his muscles and called in a croaking voice to Joseph Moore. There was no answer.

He could see Miss Keough still in a kneeling position on the upper berth, hunched over as though to protect herself from the sea. The movements of the ship did not move her because she was frozen to the berth.

It was very unsettling.

A thought struck him: how long had he slept? Hours? Minutes? Had everybody been rescued while he slept?

Kieley eased himself stiffly from the closet and dropped to the floor, gasping in shock as the icy water surged up around his chest. Moving hurriedly before it paralyzed him completely, he waded from the room. He shouted, "Mr. Moore! Mr. Moore! Hallo-o-o!" But his voice was lost in the ceaseless din of ship and sea.

"Is *anybody* here?" he called, groping into the cross-alleyway. Still shouting, he floundered into John

Munn's room. There was less water here. The inner walls had collapsed but the wardrobe was intact and quite dry inside. He spied a bowler hat and tentatively tried it on. It fitted well enough, but he placed it back on the berth.

Kieley went back into the alleyway. The seas rolled through and on into the social hall, and he stared into it with a feeling of revulsion. The port wall had caved in, the floor and the ceiling had collapsed into a twisted mass of jagged steel and wood, the sea tumbled through the ceiling, wreckage pounded against the starboard wall.

There was certainly no escape that way. He explored the cross-alleyway and found the linen closet. It was still comparatively dry, though bitterly cold. Whether Moore had escaped through the skylight he did not know, but it was a way out. He cupped his hands around his mouth and shouted, "Hallo-o-o! Hallo-o-o! Come and save me! Hallo-o-o!"

He heard no answering shouts, and the thought nagged at him that everyone might have been taken off, leaving him alone.

He shouted until his voice grew hoarse; then, exhausted by the exertion and cold, he rested.

The men in the fiddley heard Kieley and did their best to make contact, but the seas constantly sweeping the deck would have carried them away if they had tried to reach him through the skylight. They shouted back at him, but their voices were snatched by the wind and drowned by the noise of the ship.

Presently Kieley began to shout again, his voice cracking with despair, and James, at great risk, lay on the deck and stuck his head into the skylight, shouting: "We'll get you out by-and-by, Mr. Kieley; don't worry."

He did not know if Kieley heard, but the seas were

rushing upon him and he scurried for the fiddley.

Kieley had heard. Satisfied that he would not be left behind, he returned to the comparative comfort of his room and climbed back into the dry wardrobe.

In the ventilator immediately forward of the smoke-stack, Noah Dauphinee was cramped, numb and so cold that all feeling was gone from his body. His feet, without the protection of boots, were dead stumps. The suction of the seas in the stokehold below created an icy draft in the ventilator, compounding his misery.

From his perch he had a grandstand view of the destruction below. He had witnessed the last few survivors reeling to the Marconi house, and the deck was a millpond compared to the fury of tumbling white water around the *Florizel*. Most horrible of all were the bodies of the dead, their limbs flopping as they rolled around on the deck. Many were nearly nude, others were fully dressed, but all were being battered to pulp.

Kitty Cantwell and Minnie Denief had not seen or spoken to one another. There were so many people crammed in the small room that it had not been possible to move about or change position. All body senses had been deadened by the bitter cold, and they existed in a timeless other-world of unreality. Only John Johnston remained cheerful and encouraging with his little jokes and lively banter.

Beside him, Charlie Reelis began to shake uncontrollably, "I'm dying," he muttered.

Johnston grabbed him, rubbed him vigorously, and slapped his face. "You're not dying, Charlie, you're all right," he said. "Come on now, ol' man, we'll be out of here soon."

The survivors watched and listened apathetically as Johnston energetically massaged the shivering man.

They were too detached to care whether Reelis lived or died.

Under Johnston's determined ministrations, Reelis slowly revived. He stopped shaking, the color came back to his cheeks. "Thanks," he muttered.

The fiddley was a miserable place, made more so by the wind whooshing through the floor grating.

Cleary, clad only in singlet and pants, felt no physical discomfort. Sullivan, fully dressed, with the added protection of his greatcoat, felt immeasurably cold. Finally, unable to stand the continual draft, he dashed for the Marconi house, pushed the door open, and squeezed inside. As wet and cheerless as it was, there was the illusion of warmth in the crowd.

Then Maloney died, his body sagging against those around him. There was no doubt that he was dead, and the decision was made to put him outside in order to let a survivor in from the fiddley. The decision was agreed upon with universal relief, and with great difficulty they maneuvered the body through the crowd, to the door, and placed it outside on the deck where the seas swept it away.

Jackman was a monstrous sight with his bandaged, battered face peering from the depths of the blanket Johnston had wrapped around him, but his injuries did not deter him from trying to execute his duties. He took command now and bellowed to those in the fiddley: "We can get another man in the Marconi room now."

Cleary, followed by a determined Sparrow, dashed across the deck. Both managed to get inside somehow.

The little room was standing up admirably under the continual bombardment of the sea, although the split in the roof had widened. The pillow Johnston had stuffed into the gap was sodden and dripping, but it still checked the downpour.

Jimmy Dwyer, his shinbone throbbing fiercely from the crack he had received, was holding the door when a great wave wrenched it off its hinges. Those grouped by the opening were suddenly exposed to the full force of the water rushing inside. Lethargy disappeared, there were groans and cries, and the people shrank closer together, as though by doing so the sea could not touch them. Dwyer could not stand it. He hopped across the deck toward the fiddley to join Mate James, Burnham, Moore, and José Fernandez. Sullivan followed.

Fernandez looked as if he would die any second, but they continued to take turns rubbing and breathing on him.

Inside the Marconi room, there were shrieks of fear. The ones receiving the full impact of the sea were in danger of being sucked outside, and Johnston shouted, "We'll have to take up the carpet and nail it over the door."

Clumsily maneuvering the survivors, Johnston and the two wireless operators pried the carpet off the floor. Carter produced a few nails from somewhere, and tacked the thick rug over the doorway. It was sodden, but it was heavy enough to break the seas a bit.

Mate James continued to watch for signs of rescue, but there was still no trace of smoke on the horizon. He thought of Martin and Dooley. Had they tried that swim to the beach? Were they still alive? He did not have much hope that they were.

James and Sullivan took turns dodging in and out of the fiddley to wave at the men on the beach. It was dangerous, but it was important to let those ashore know they were still alive. The other men remained under the canvas with Fernandez. They had effectively closed their minds to the horror of the bodies beating about the deck, but now and again speculated about the man in the ventilator. Who was he? They could even see the humor of it when he poked a cautious head out of the cowl for a look around.

Sometime between 2:00 and 4:00 P.M., James noticed that the sea was calming a little. It was caused, he knew, by the ebb tide running against the sea. At the same time his attention was caught by activity on the far shore beneath Burnt Head. A handful of men were clustered around a dory ready to take advantage of the ebbing tide. "They're trying to launch a dory," he shouted. They jammed the fiddley opening to watch four men run the dory into the boiling surf. If one dory could make it, others would quickly follow and rescue would be effected. But the dory up-ended and turned over. "It was a good try," James said.

His eyes scanned the horizon. Where were the rescue ships? If they had been on the scene at this moment during the ebb tide, he felt sure they would have been able to take the survivors off the wreck without difficulty.

*Where were they?*

In the forecastle, Martin clutched the framework of the doorway to keep from being washed away. As he had estimated, the ebb tide had flattened the seas a little, but it was not humanly possible to secure the lines that were in the bow; no man could withstand the force of those seas tunneling in under the forecastle head.

Dooley asked, "Do we swim ashore, Cap'n?"

Pinsent was horrified. "Cap'n, you can't swim ashore in that — it ain't *that* smooth."

"I tell you, it is madness," Ledingham said with severity. "Think of your wife and children."

Martin *was* thinking about his family. He had thoughts, too, about other things in the past few hours. Whatever the cause of the wreck, *he* had to answer for it. Whatever the cost, *he* had to accept the blame. He looked at the sea for a long time. It should have been considerably calmer with the ebb tide and the offshore wind, but it was still ugly and intimidating. He had no intention of foolishly throwing away his life even if his career was in ruins. If the sea did not calm sufficiently for him to be reasonably sure of survival, he would wait for rescue.

Meanwhile, like James and Sullivan in the fiddley, Martin and his crew in the forecastle darted out between seas to wave to the people on the shore.

It was mid-afternoon when the train chugged into Renews, where horses and carts were waiting to take the rescue team to the beach at Cappahayden. The wind was brisk, and it was a cold, rough ride as they jolted over the frozen cliffs to the hillock at the very tip of Horn Head. It was around 4:00 P.M. when they got there.

They looked with horror and grief upon the *Florizel*, smothered in a cradle of wild white water exploding against her smokestack and bow. The seas were running through her and over her. She was a complete and total wreck. They could hear the frenzied rattle of her hull, the shriek of her torn plates, as the brutal seas forced her, like a battering ram, over the rocks. The Honourable Tasker Cook could scarcely believe that there were still survivors aboard. "Is it possible?" he asked a burly, wind-burned fisherman.

The fisherman assured him that it was. "There's some in the bow of 'er, and we seen someone by the smokestack. They come out now and again and waves to us."

"Can't we *do* anything?" Cook asked.

"We can wait, sir, and that's all we can do," the fisherman replied.

The cut into the main telegraph line had been made, and Bowring's operator set up his apparatus on the hillock. Soon he was transmitting the grim details of the wreck back to St. John's. Marshall was already setting up the rocket apparatus.

The official party looked around the wreckage-strewn beach. Solid mahogany doors, furniture, wooden walls, the hatch of number-three hold and the ship's rigging jumbled the shoreline with broken casks of herring, lobster, and fish oil. Eight bodies had been laid in the shelter of the hillock.

The dead who had washed ashore were Second Officer John King, Second Steward Charlie Snow, Waiter Stanley Squires, Mrs. W. F. Butler, C. H. Miller, Edgar Froude, W. E. Bishop, and George Long. The body of Mrs. Butler was clad only in night apparel. The sea had wrested the fur coat from her body.

# CHAPTER 20

*MATE JAMES* saw the first rocket fired. He noted the sparks as it was launched, and wondered where they had found such an apparatus. The rocket fell short of the wreck by fifty or more feet; a second rocket, a short time later, fell on the bow of the *Florizel* but was immediately swept overboard.

Dusk was falling and no more lines were fired.

The dancing fires on the beach were of little comfort to the men in the fiddley. Just four hours from the port of St. John's with its fleet of ships, and not one of them was in sight eleven hours after an s.o.s. had been sent out.

It was incomprehensible.

In the forecastle they were unaware of rescue attempts; able to dash outside only for brief seconds at a time, they observed nothing. Joseph Burry, poking around the little room, produced two tiny oil lanterns. They were preposterously small and not designed to give a great deal of light, but it was better than no light at all. "We won't be in the dark," he said, producing matches that were miraculously dry.

Somehow, the two dim lights helped.

Noah Dauphinee, in the ventilator for nearly twelve hours, could not bear it any longer. If it meant risking his life to get to the Marconi house, he was going to risk it. He was stiff and clumsy and his feet were quite lifeless, but he got out of the ventilator cowl, lowered himself over the side of the fiddley casing, and made it to the Marconi house, pushing through the sodden carpet into the cold, wet, crowded little room.

To the survivors it seemed as if they had been on the wrecked ship a lifetime. Strangely enough, the majority felt neither the cold, hunger, nor thirst; most of them philosophically awaited their fate. There was still prayer, with Kitty leading the Rosary in a good, strong voice. Other times it was Cecil Carter. Hymns of praise were sung with much feeling, and in between there was John Johnston with his little nonsense jokes. But mainly, they waited.

The rescue ships had labored through the heavily packed sish ice. The *Home* and the *Gordon C* finally steamed out of it roughly a dozen miles north of Cappahayden, and were plunging through heavy seas, with the *Gordon C* edging ahead of the *Home* in the race to the wreck. The old *Terra Nova*, lagging in the rear, thumped along, rolling and pitching when she left the sanctuary of the icefield.

Great waves piled steeply on the Bantems, thundering landward to crash on the shore in a magnificent display of flying spindrift, streaming off the rocks and ledges in a myriad of waterfalls. It was heavy going for the old ship and she labored tremendously. Captain Nicholas Kennedy stared over the angry ocean and came to the conclusion that there would be no rescue work until the seas quietened somewhat; meanwhile, he had better take the old ship to a place of shelter. Renews was the nearest harbor to Cappahayden; he decided it would be best to shelter there.

The *Hawk*, out of port only a couple of hours, belched heavy black smoke as she plowed through the ice just south of Cape Spear. Captain Marcus Simonsen still seethed with impatience.

The wind and the sea were moderating at last. The *Florizel's* movements seemed less violent; the overpowering boom of the angry surf was decreasing slightly in volume. The survivors' spirits dared to lift a little.

Mate James, keeping constant vigil, saw the glimmer of ships' lights coming down the coast. "They're coming!" he bawled to those in the fiddley. "They're coming!"

The *Gordon C*, with all lights blazing, arrived at dusk. From the bridge Perry could see the line of breakers gleaming against the dark bulk of the land, and the hulk of the *Florizel* showing intermittently through the welter of breaking seas. Golden fires glimmering on the beach beyond the surf cast streamers of reflected light over the water.

Captain Perry eased his ship to within a hundred and fifty yards of the wreck, close enough to observe that the stern had obviously broken off and that the seas were passing over and through her.

"She's finished," he muttered.

It was too rough to launch a boat for a closer look, and too rough to anchor this close to shore. He backed his ship off.

"See any sign of life?" he asked his crew.

"There can't be anyone alive aboard that one, Cap'n."

They watched and waited, but the *Florizel* appeared to be a desolate ruin.

The *Home*, with the Honourable John Stone aboard,

steamed onto the scene at approximately six o'clock. Captain Spracklin had eased her in as close as he dared, but she was a larger ship than the *Gordon C* and he prudently kept her offshore by a good mile. The moon was rising, though it was not yet dark, and they could clearly see the wreck. The remains of a lifeboat hanging from the davits on the far side was plainly visible, but there was no sign of life.

With mixed emotions, they kept watch, and after about an hour of close observation, the *Gordon C* steamed around the stern of the *Home* and the two captains consulted. "I'm sure there's nobody alive on her," Perry shouted.

"It looks very much like it," Spracklin shouted back.

The ocean was unpleasantly turbulent, and there was nothing they could do. "There's too much sea for me to anchor here. I'm going to go back to Fermeuse and send in a report to St. John's. We'll be back before daybreak," Perry shouted.

Backing off, the *Gordon C* headed back along the coast to the quiet shelter of Fermeuse, seven to eight miles from the scene of the wreck. The *Terra Nova* had, meantime, taken shelter in Renews harbor.

As Perry steamed away, Captain Spracklin suggested to Stone, "Perhaps we should go, too, and send back a report to St. John's."

Stone had other plans. "It's a nice moonlight night, Captain; the wind and sea seem to be going down a little. I think it will be all right to anchor off here so that we can be on the spot bright and early," he said.

Captain Spracklin did not argue. He ordered a sounding and let the anchor down. The Minister of Marine and Fisheries hunched over the rail, watching the wreck, the lights and the sea, and presently he made a decision. "I want you to let me have a boat to go in close to the *Florizel*," he told the captain.

If Captain Spracklin had time to think of the repercussions that could follow if a Minister of the Government of Newfoundland should lose his life while attempting rescue operations, he dared not dwell on them. John Stone was not a man to be deterred from his purpose, and he did not expect any question about his decision. The firm jaw, the direct gaze, the solid build, indicated competency and authority.

Spracklin ordered a lifeboat lowered, and presently Stone, accompanied by naval reservists Walter Reid, Samuel Cooper, and Edgar Button, pushed off from the *Home*. "Be careful!" Spracklin bawled to the seamen.

Stone ordered, "Proceed."*

The sea was a confusion of white-capped peaks and shadowed valleys. Spray flew over them, hitting their skins like pellets; black ocean streaked with white rose and fell around them, but the brawny sailors pulled up hill, down valley, until they got to within a hundred yards of the wreck. In the shallow water their lifeboat was in danger of swamping.

The *Florizel* looked stark and dead, and she clanked noisily on the rocks. Cooper, a seaman to the core, couldn't help but wonder how Captain Martin had gotten his ship into such an unlikely spot. Would his own good luck have saved him again if he had sailed on her?

"Can you get closer?" shouted Stone.

Cautiously, keeping the boat head on to the swells, they eased closer. In the moonlight the fiddley and the Marconi house were clearly detailed, but there was no sign of life. The minister cupped his hands around his mouth and called, "Hallo-o-o! *Florizel*!"

His voice was lost in the uproar. "Shout with me," he ordered the seamen, and they shouted long and vigorously, but it was a feeble contest they waged with the

---

* Stone's active participation in the rescue was not discovered until after the enquiry, and it was never publicized.

sea. There was no answering call, no indication of life aboard.

Stone did not give up. "Even if they do hear us, they can't expose themselves to the sea," he told his companions.

They scanned the ship for signs of life. Beyond the *Florizel*, small fires danced on the beach, their reflections sparkling on the black seas outside the wreck. Stone was concentrating on two dim lights on the bow of the *Florizel* when one of the men yelled, "There's a light near the smokestack. Look at it."

They saw a light winking, but the fires on the beach winked too, so that it was difficult to know what they were looking at. Stone shouted back, "It looks like a light all right, but it could be a reflection of the lights from the beach." His attention went back to the bow. "Do you see the lights on her bow?"

They looked, but were not convinced. "I don't think there's any light there, sir," Reid said.

The Minister was a very determined man. "Let us see if we can find out. Can we drift close enough to make sure?"

They eased the lifeboat in and rowed back and forth, their eyes riveted on the ship. Eventually they came to the conclusion that the two lights were a faint diffusion of light emanating from two of the portholes in the bow. Again they hailed the *Florizel*, daring to go even closer, though their boat rocked dangerously in the great turbulence closer to the wreck, but there was no response to their calls.

"The lights are there, somebody has to be aboard," Stone said.

"It could be the oil lamps that were burning when she struck, sir," Cooper said.

That had not occurred to Stone. Logically, it could be any of the little oil lamps that had been burning when she struck before dawn, and it was conceivable that they were still burning in the forecastle where the sea could not reach them. He was of a mind to accept this, but to be absolutely sure he ordered them to row back and forth several more times, shouting until their voices were hoarse. There was no indication of life whatever, and finally they returned to the *Home*.

It was now 8:00 P.M.

Captain Spracklin was skeptical about the lights. "It *had* to be the reflection of the fires on shore," he said. "Look at 'em."

It was true. The ocean around the *Florizel* was alive with sparkling lights cast by the fires that danced attendance on the dead hulk.

Stone knew the lights were aboard, but they could do nothing until the seas abated. Meanwhile, the *Gordon C* had steamed into the harbor of Fermeuse and sent reports to St. John's to the effect that the *Florizel* was totally wrecked with the seas going over her; that it had been impossible to board her and there had been no sign of life.

Though he had been keeping constant vigil, Mate James had not seen the lifeboat from the *Home* nor heard the men when they tried to make contact. Major Sullivan, using his flashlight sparingly to preserve the batteries, let it wink now and again in the direction of the ship to let them know there were survivors. José Fernandez, huddling under the canvas, was still alive.

In the forecastle, Burry and Pinsent had found two sodden packages of Grape Nuts cereal and a half-bottle of whisky diluted with sea water. Standing watch in the doorway when the seas permitted, they all nibbled on the cereal and wet their lips with the whisky. During the break between seas, they took turns dashing outside to wave one of the little lanterns to the people on the beach. It was a risky undertaking on the sloping, icy deck, and there was no time to explore the situation seaward; they were, therefore, not aware that rescue ships were on the scene or that a lifeboat had tried to make contact.

The *Hawk* arrived on the scene about 9:00 P.M. Only the *Home* was there, anchored a mile offshore. Simonsen did not waste time speculating about the whereabouts of the *Gordon C* or the *Terra Nova*; after a grim look at the wreck, he steamed within hailing distance of the *Home*. "Were you in yet?" he shouted.

Leaning over the ship's bridge, Spracklin shouted back, "We had a boat in, but there's no sign of life. Nothing."

Simonsen could not accept that. The heavy seas sweeping the hull, the death watch kept by the people of Cappahayden, made his throat constrict for the gallant ship. Every instinct told him that no human could withstand the terrible force of the sea for the length of time the *Florizel* had been wrecked — but he had to find out for himself. He bellowed to Captain Spracklin, "I'm going in."

Simonsen maneuvered the *Hawk* as close to the wreck as he dared, but twice they were swept northward by the reversed inshore current, which Simonsen estimated as flowing a swift two to three knots. Finally, he ordered the anchor dropped and a lifeboat lowered. Offshore, the seas were flattening a little, but they remained dangerously steep and the boat rocked wildly. Under the expert oarsmanship of Martin Dalton and naval reservist Dan Ralph, the boat eased toward the *Florizel*, getting as close as Stone and his men had earlier. Though the moonlight clearly etched the appalling details of the wreck, they saw no sign of life, and duly reported so to Simonsen.

He still would not believe all had been lost. "We'll soon see if anyone's aboard," he said, and ordered anchor up. The tough little whaler moved forward, her crew sounding continually to warn of sudden shoaling. "Send up a rocket or two," Simonsen bawled, and hauled on the whistle.

With her whistle shrilling and rockets shooting in the sky, the *Hawk* dropped anchor dangerously close to the wreck. There was an answering light from the *Florizel's* smokestack, and Simonsen jubilantly ordered another lifeboat out. Again the heavy seas prevented the sailors from getting close enough to hail the survivors.

Frustrated, the men returned to their ship.

Mary Jackman sat by her window staring out into the bright night. She saw and heard nothing, was unaware of the passing time; her mind let her see only Phil's smiling face. Mrs. Drover volunteered to stay up with her, to give her comfort and share her grief, but Mary, unwilling to accept comfort or to acknowledge grief, stared fixedly out the window, heedless of the kindly ministrations of her friend, who finally gave up and quietly dozed.

The priest had been to see her earlier. "Mary, you must accept the will of God," he had said gently.

Fiercely she had rejected it. "Please don't start *that*, Father. I'm doing the best I can; don't give me sympathy."

He had stayed only a little while.

She had received no news that Phil was lost, therefore she sat and waited for him. Her thoughts were on him with such intensity that she could almost feel his presence in the room with her.

Dora Crocker was convinced that the ball of fire she had seen the evening before had been a token of evil, a sign

212

of death, and she knew in her bones that George was dead.

Amy did not believe in such things, and tried to persuade her mother that it was nonsense. "It's just superstition, Mother," she said.

"I feel it. I *know* it," Dora whispered, her face ravaged with sorrow. She and George had been too close for her not to know.

Upstairs, the baby whimpered and Amy was there to tend to the needs of her little sister. She had her own griefs and fears for her father and for Joe, but her mother, in her terrible grief, took precedence over everything else.

Relatives and friends had taken charge of the Maloney family, cushioning the shock as the news from the telegraph office grew worse by the hour. Mary Maloney was curiously detached, as if she had been emotionally immunized by the terror of the night before. She did not weep or fluctuate between hope and despair, but kept busy in spite of relatives and friends.

Her concern was for the children, the older ones especially, who understood the magnitude of the disaster and the possible consequences. They were very brave, but seemed to need the comfort of her presence, and their need, somehow, bolstered her own courage.

# CHAPTER 21

*WHEN THE Hawk's* whistle blew and rockets lit up the sky, the survivors in the Marconi room were momentarily bereft of speech. Then there was a burst of excitement; lethargy disappeared and thirty-two bodies squirmed and stretched in the tiny room; heads craned toward the cracked portholes.

"Thank God!"

"At last!"

"Saved! We're going to be saved!"

Some were expectant of immediate deliverance. "How long will it be before they take us off?"

Jackman cautioned: "It'll be a while yet."

"It won't be long, will it?" a voice pleaded.

Carter took his flashlight from his pocket. "I'll try to signal them and find out."

They waited eagerly as he tried to signal through the porthole, then he announced: "The batteries are dead. We'll just have to wait."

They groaned.

The moon cast its cold light in through the portholes, and the pale outlines of their faces hung like disembodied apparitions above the crush of bodies. When the combers rose menacingly and blocked the light, someone lifted a crucifix as if to ward off the danger.

It was impossible to sustain such a pitch of expectancy, and gradually spirits fell lower than ever. Johnston remained the good Samaritan, coaxing them out of their depression. "It won't be *that* long," he told them.

In his room below, Kieley was aware only of the ceaseless noise. Occasionally he went to the skylight and shouted, just to hear the sound of human voices. "We'll get you out, Mr. Kieley," he was assured.

Each time he returned to his room, careful not to look at the frozen form of Miss Keough in the upper berth, and climbed back into the closet.

The *Home* and the *Hawk* lay to, Simonsen on the *Hawk* impatiently waiting for the seas to moderate; the *Gordon C* had not returned and there had been no sign of the old *Terra Nova*. Then about 1:00 A.M. with lights blazing, the *Prospero* arrived. Bowring's message had been waiting for her at Marystown when she arrived there that morning at eleven-thirty, and she had turned around and steamed posthaste to the wreck. Her chief steward, Charlie Miller, was in an agony of suspense over the fate of his son, James.

Captain Stephen Parsons quickly surveyed the situation. The fires on the beach pinpointed the wreck and he steamed slowly inside the *Home*, blasting his whistle continuously to alert the survivors and easing his ship cautiously inshore until he was almost as close to the wreck as the little *Hawk*, practically on the edge of the breakers tumbling on the shore. Playing his powerful searchlight on the wreck, he ordered the ship's lifeboat and mail launch out.

The other ships followed suit, blasting their whistles, filling the night with musical discord, and launching their dories and lifeboats.

The *Prospero's* lifeboat was manned by Chief Engineer

James McKinley, Bos'un William Crocker, Steward A. Starkes, Fireman W. Ashman, Donkeyman W. O'Toole, and passenger George Hiscock, a private in the Royal Newfoundland Regiment.

From all points they converged on the wreck. The searchlight showed in stark detail the ravaged deck, the seas rushing over the hull.

"Easy!"

"Hard over!"

Fragments of voices could be heard over the sound of the sea as the dorymen closed in around her. Circling the stern, they rowed cautiously to the lee of her.

The dory, renowned for its extraordinary capabilities in riding heavy seas and surf, was only as good as those who manned it. These men were Newfoundlanders, born to the sea, Grand Bank fishermen before the war, and experts in a dory. Closer they maneuvered, a hairsbreadth from disaster as cresting seas hung over them before a twist on an oar veered the dory away. Deep in the trough one moment, lifting skyward the next, they closed in.

The lifeboat of the *Prospero* was manipulated right to the *Florizel*; then it rose on the crest of a wave and capsized when its bow got caught in the railing. Her crew plunged overboard, Ashman even touching bottom as he was sucked under. Fortunately they wore lifebelts, and struggled to the wild, milky surface to find that their boat, with its air-sealed compartments, had righted itself; it was awash and rocking sluggishly up the side of a wave. To a man they made for it.

O'Toole climbed aboard first, then Ashman, Crocker, Sparkes, and Hiscock; McKinley clambered over the stern. Before they had time to organize, a sea broke under the boat, capsizing it again. This time it remained bottom up. Struggling against the numbing cold and the strong backwash from the wreck, they again made it to the lifeboat, clung to its bottom for a moment to catch their breath. The shock of the icy water had mercifully numbed their bodies. "We've got to turn it over," Mc-Kinley yelled.

With limbs that were stiffening, they strove mightily to right the boat.

"Now!" roared McKinley.

They heaved, and the boat rolled upright. But a sea curled over, burying the lifeboat and capsizing it again.

The six men were too exhausted to do anything more, and they were barely able to keep their heads above the waves. The *Hawk's* dory with Dalton, Pope, and Ralph and the crew in the *Prospero's* mail launch discovered what was happening, and simultaneously came to their rescue. The dory crew hauled McKinley out of the water; the others were pulled into the mail launch. The dory made for the *Hawk*; the mail launch made for the *Prospero* with the lifeboat in tow. McKinley was given a bracing drink of rum and a change of clothing, then rowed back to his own ship.

The accident halted rescue operations temporarily.

Unaware of the drama that had happened practically beside them, people in the Marconi room were reaching a fever pitch of excitement again as Carter, looking through the porthole, described the glorious sight of three ships' lights trailing quicksilver pathways across the sea.

"Are they *coming*?" someone asked impatiently.

"Can you see them?"

"Will it be long?" Kitty asked.

"I can only see the ships," he told them.

Major Sullivan pushed into the Marconi room. "Where's the Marconi operator?" he asked.

"Here."

"I have a flashlight you can use to contact the other

operators, if you wish to do so."

Carter reached for it eagerly. "My own flashlight is dead," he told Sullivan.

"The batteries in this one are going too, but there should be enough juice for a few messages."

"We'll give it a try, Major."

The flashlight was passed over the crowd, and placing it against the porthole, Carter winked out a message in Morse:

*"Are you coming aboard?"*

Like every other person aboard the *Prospero*, Operator Jim Myrick had been rooted to the rail, unable to tear his eyes from the wreck. Reading the message winking faintly from the black hulk, he ran to the bridge and relayed it to Captain Parsons. Parsons, unaware that the lifeboat and mail launch were returning, commanded: "Use the whistle and tell him two of our boats have gone in, and ask him how many are aboard."

Myrick did as he was ordered, and with the ship's deep-throated whistle, replied in Morse:

*"Two of our boats are near you now. How many aboard?"*

The little light winked back:

*"Forty."*

Incredulously Myrick told the captain, "Forty. He says forty survivors, sir."

Parsons found that difficult to believe. "Are you *sure* that's what he said?"

Myrick was not sure. The little light, winking amidst the other sparkling reflections of the fires, was a poor one, and he knew he could easily have been mistaken. "I'll ask again, sir."

The *Prospero's* whistle, reverberating under the hills of Cappahayden, blasted in Morse:

*"Forty. Please repeat."*

Barely distinguishable, the light winked again:

*"Forty."*

"It's forty, sir," Myrick reported.

They could hardly believe it.

Carter passed the news to the others. "The *Prospero* says two of her boats are near us now. We'll soon be saved."

There was a stir, a few croaking cheers, and more craning of heads toward the portholes. "The sea will be smoother on the starboard side; that's where they'll come in for us," Jackman told them.

Those near the starboard portholes peered out through, trying to pick up a glimpse of the lifeboats on the dark sea. "Well . . . ?" someone asked, voice rising anxiously.

They saw nothing.

Gunner Hatchard offered, "Give me the flashlight and I'll go outside and guide them in."

Carter gave him the flashlight and Hatchard darted outside. It was a dangerous task, for the seas were rolling right up over the ship, and if he slipped on the icy deck, he was finished. Hugging the shelter of the smokestack, he darted as far aft as he dared, grabbing at a funnel stay to anchor himself. There was no sign of the smaller boats supposed to be close to the wreck but he flicked the light on and off, waved it back and forth, eyes raking the seas for an answering light, ears attentive for the sound of a hail. He saw and heard nothing, and presently, drenched and frozen, he dashed back to the Marconi room.

The dorymen had not seen the winking light or learned of the number of survivors aboard; they were too busy coping with the seas as they made their way back to their ships.

But one dory was returning. Marcus Simonsen, unable to stand the inactivity, had ordered a dory out, and with Martin Dalton and Michael Whelan, was stroking toward the wreck. They got to within a cable's length of her and dared not go closer; their dory, pitching wildly, was kept upright only by the expert oarsmanship of the crew. Simonsen cupped his hands around his mouth and bellowed, "Ahoy-y-y-y! *Florizel!*"

This time, alerted to the activity of the rescue boats, James and those in the fiddley, shouted back in unison.

"How many aboard?" Simonsen shouted.

A disembodied voice roared over the noise and it sounded as if it said: "Fourteen!"

"Did he say fourteen?" Simonsen asked.

They all agreed that was what they had heard, but decided it would be foolhardy to try and get closer. "We can't help 'em yet," Simonsen conceded.

Back on the *Hawk*, he ordered the anchor up and daringly positioned the whaler even closer to the wreck. They would have to wait until daylight before anything further could be done.


Aboard the *Prospero*, Chief Steward Charlie Miller wished desperately to know if his son was alive. He asked Myrick, "Would you ask the *Florizel* if Jim Miller is alive?"

Myrick laboriously tooted:

*"Is Jim Miller alive?"*

Carter, who had the names of those in the Marconi room and the fiddley, winked back the information that Miller was not among them, but the flashlight batteries were failing rapidly and Myrick had to report, "I can't make it out, Charlie, the light is too weak."

Miller was left in suspense.

About 4:00 A.M. the *Gordon C* steamed back on the scene. The *Terra Nova* was close behind.


The seas were moderating quickly and there was great activity aboard the wreck. She rattled still, but her movements were quieter. Hobbling on frostbitten feet,

Captain Martin, Dooley, Pinsent, and Burry helped the crippled Alex Ledingham over the wreckage to the Marconi room.

Lumsden gave a glad shout: "Cap'n Martin! We thought you an' Dooley were lost, sir."

Martin wasted no time. They could move freely about the deck now, and a few bits and pieces of rope that had so providentially come to hand earlier were secured and lifelines rigged. Martin himself rigged a safety line from the Marconi house to the davits on the starboard side in anticipation of rescue from that quarter. The seas were still rough, but in the lee of the wreck they were reasonably moderate.

"We're ready when they are," he said.

"Mr. Kieley is still below, Cap'n," Mate James told him.

"Then we'd better get him out."

"He comes to the skylight now and then; we're waiting for him."

Below, Kieley was suddenly aware that the noise had lessened considerably. The frozen form of Margaret Keough was a dim blur on the upper berth, but he averted his eyes as he eased himself once more into the icy water and waded into the linen closet. "Hallo-o-o! Is anyone aboard?" he yelled.

Captain Martin stuck his head over the skylight. "Stand by, Mr. Kieley, we'll have you out in a jiffy."

In a short time Mate James, gunners Hatchard and Curtis, and Joseph Moore stood over the skylight. They lowered a piece of strong line through the skylight and gave him orders to hitch it under his arms. The black seas in the pantry shaft sucked and hissed when he jumped as directed, but the men caught him and hauled him to the deck.

"Thank God I see living human beings again," he said as they assisted him to the Marconi house.

# CHAPTER 22

*IT WAS* not yet daybreak when dories and lifeboats from all five ships began to converge on the wreck, the Minister of Marine and Fisheries amongst them in the *Home's* lifeboat. The *Prospero's* two boats were under the command of two passengers, Captain Eugene Burden, and Captain William Windsor, of the Merchant Navy. They had been bound for the Burin Peninsula on the south coast to bring a ship to St. John's.

Captain Spracklin had no intention of risking another near-fatal accident; this time both boats were equipped with lifebelts, anchors, and lifelines of various weights. He told Eugene Burden, "Moor the lifeboat as close to the wreck as possible, and try to get a lifeline aboard so the smaller boats can warp back and forth."

Burden nodded, and Spracklin continued, "You're going to be practically in the middle of the breakers, so the mail launch will stand by to rescue you if your boat should swamp."

The seas were still mountainous in the shoal water surrounding the wreck; swells rolled continually over her, combers reared occasionally and raced the length of her, and she still clanked.

The rescuers began to close in, the unwieldy lifeboats taking the lead. Poised on the wave crests, dropping in the black troughs, they bobbed up and down like partners in a dance. Wary of breaching seas, they inched forward.

Suddenly the dory with Captain Perry and his engineer, Robert Pierson, caught the crest of a steep wave that half filled her. Neither Perry nor Pierson — nor any of the dorymen for that matter — wore lifebelts, having discarded them for more freedom of movement, and they had to bail furiously. The others could not see what was happening, but the wild motions of their dories urged caution, and they eased off. As the sky lightened, they began to move in again.

Offshore, the ocean was quietening and the surf at the shoreline was less ferocious. In a little while, the dories of the Cappahayden fishermen were launched from the beach, without mishap this time, to join the little fleet of boats approaching the wreck.

The *Prospero's* lifeboat dropped anchor about fifty yards from the *Florizel*, while Perry and Pierson, back in action, were much closer, trying to throw a lifeline aboard. This line was too heavy and it repeatedly fell short of the wreck.

They rowed to the lifeboat. "You got a lighter line than ours?" Perry asked Burden.

Burden passed them a lighter one. "When you get it aboard, bring it back to us. We'll tie it to a heavier line, and when they set it up, you can haul yourself in to the *Florizel*," he told Perry.

"Done!" Perry said.

This line was too light and the wind carried it away until Perry attached an oarlock to the end of it, and on the next throw, it landed on the wreck. Mate James rushed from the smokestack and secured it firmly amid the cheers of the people on the beach. Perry rowed back to the lifeboat with his end of the line, which Burden knotted to a heavier one; James hauled away until he had the thick, strong lifeline tied to a stanchion. The line stretched low over the heaving water, and the dories gathered by the lifeboat. "You can haul yourselves to the *Florizel* now," Burden shouted.

Perry and Pierson were the first to pull themselves hand over hand to the wreck. The dory skittered and yawed, but finally the men were clinging to the edge of the boat deck where Captain Martin was waiting for them. "Who's to go first?" Perry yelled.

"We have two women," Martin called back.

Kitty Cantwell was first. She had a glimpse of the hundreds of people lining the beach and heard the cheers as she approached the edge. The dory, wallowing in the trough, looked like it was a long way down, then it was leaping upward and Perry held up his arms, shouting, "Jump!"

Obediently she jumped and landed in his arms.

The sea combed up and they hurriedly pushed off until it rushed over and beyond. Minnie Denief was waiting when they eased back alongside. She jumped when commanded, and Perry decided to take them immediately to the *Gordon C.*

Terrified by the seas rearing over the little dory, Kitty quavered, "Are we safe?"

Perry replied, "You're as safe as if you were in God's vest pocket, ma'am."

It was a nightmare journey through brutal, uncivil seas before the two young women were safely aboard the *Gordon C.*

One after the other, the dories made it to the wreck on the lifeline, taking off a couple of survivors at a time and delivering them to the *Hawk*, sixty yards away. It was a slow process because only one boat at a time could go in, but the rescue continued in orderly fashion until the crew of number-one dory of the *Terra Nova*, with Charles W. Penney, Adolphus Morey, and Harold Clouter, grew impatient. Ignoring the lifeline, they stroked through the seas that threatened to overwhelm and destroy their little boat, and with heroic effort, eventually positioned her alongside the *Florizel*. This crew would later be credited with rescuing twenty-three of the forty-four survivors. Utterly indifferent to their own safety, they rowed like men possessed, smartly delivering the survivors to the *Hawk*. Dr. J. G. Knowlton, on the bridge of the *Terra Nova* with Captain Kennedy, watched in wordless admiration.

Another dory with Matt Shanahan, Pat Gallagher, and George Westcott had brought eight survivors to the *Hawk* before they shipped a sea that forced them out of service. Still another was sucked under a wave and almost completely inundated. Her crew had to concentrate on saving their own lives. Both dories made it to the *Hawk* and the men went below for a change of clothing.

The Honourable John Stone, in the lifeboat crewed by Captain M. Day, Samuel Cooper, Walter Reid, Edgar Button, and Walter Nash, watched the crews going in. Under great physical strain for hours, some of the dory crews were totally exhausted. Samuel Cooper and Walter Reid took over a dory, reached the wreck, took off two men, and delivered them to the *Hawk*.

All was going well until Joseph Stockley jumped into a dory manned by Captain Perry and reservist Budden. A sea swept the dory against the side of the wreck, stove her side in, and flung the three men overboard. Stockley made a grab for the lifeline, caught it, and was hauled back to the wreck by Captain Martin. Perry and Budden, stunned by the impact, disappeared in the boiling sea. Martin searched frantically for them, but they were gone.

The sudden turbulence made it difficult for other dorymen to follow what was going on, and only the number-two dory of the *Terra Nova* was near enough to help. They saw Budden being carried shoreward and got to him. He was badly bruised and semiconscious when they hauled him aboard. They also searched for Perry but could not find him. Concluding that he had drowned, they took the injured man to the *Terra Nova*, where Dr. Knowlton ministered to his needs.

It was Eugene Burden in the *Prospero's* lifeboat who glimpsed Perry, clinging to a piece of the wrecked dory, drifting toward the shoals. He shouted to a dory crew waiting to go in to the wreck. "There's a man driving in the shoals, you'd better go in and get him."

The dory, manned by Cooper and Reid, bounded through the surf and Cooper grabbed Perry by the collar of his coat. Perry was unconscious and he was too heavy to lift aboard. They towed him back to the lifeboat, trying to keep his head above water, and several sailors hauled him aboard.

"He's full of water, better roll 'im," Burden ordered.

They rolled Perry over the seat until he showed signs of life, then Cooper and Reid took him to the *Home*.

In spite of the accidents, the rescue continued smoothly until a dory manned by Simonsen and Dalton was hit by a sea, causing it to fall off from the wreck. Major Sullivan, in the act of stepping aboard, plunged into the water. He still had his lifebelt on and Dalton grabbed him by the collar, yelling, "Hang on, we'll get you aboard."

But Sullivan saw another sea piling up behind them. He grabbed the gunwale and yelled: "Get a move on, there's another one coming."

They wasted no time. Towing Major Sullivan's two-hundred-pound weight behind them, they pulled like the devil to get away from the wreck. Burden and his

226

crew tried to help the big man into the boat, but his bulk, plus the lifebelt, made it an impossible task.

"How are we goin' to get you aboard, sir?" Burden asked.

Sullivan was used to emergencies. To the men in the dory he directed, "Grab my feet and tip me into a dory."

One of the dories was emptied and placed lengthwise between the lifeboat and Simonsen's dory; then, thrashing around until his feet came to the surface, Sullivan was held by the shoulders and feet as the dory was tipped on its side and he rolled out of the sea into it. Huge and dripping, he sat up and was taken to the *Hawk*.

All seventeen passengers had been removed and finally only seven crew members remained aboard the wreck: Captain Martin, Mate James, Bos'un Michael Power, William Dooley, Joseph Burry, Jacob Pinsent, and Bos'un William Molloy. The waited patiently.

The *Terra Nova's* dory, with naval reservists Hann, Moores, and Murphy, was easing to the side of the *Florizel* when a sea combed up, flipping men and dory over. Other dories homed in and fished them out.

The *Hawk's* dory, this time with Dalton, Ralph, and Whelan, now tried to reach the wreck, but the sea was in a truculent mood again, as though it had cooperated long enough. A wave rose up, stood the dory on end, and somersaulted it on top of the men. Dalton was hit but retained his senses as he struggled beneath her. The sea carried them toward the breakers, and this time the Renews dory with Ryan and the Quinlan brothers picked up the half-drowned men and brought them to the *Hawk*. Dalton was not able to do any more rescue work. Dan Ralph refused to take any of the dry clothing which was now in short supply; he simply wrung out his clothing and put it back on.

Captain Martin and his men, hugging the shelter of the smokestack, watched the dories retreating over the heaving seas. In the lifeboat, Eugene Burden ordered a dory emptied, tied it to the lifeline, and waved his arms to the men on the wreck. They dashed to the line and hauled the dory toward them. Over the sea it danced, weaving and pitching with the peculiar grace all dory-men admire, and in a few minutes it was bobbing and curtseying beneath them. Martin ordered Molloy, Burry, and Pinsent aboard. They hauled themselves to the lifeboat without incident. One more time the dory went to the wreck, and Dooley, Power, James, and Captain Martin stepped aboard, unhitched the lifeline, and left the dead ship with her grisly cargo of bodies still wedged about the deck.

It was approximately 8:00 A.M., twenty-seven hours after the *Florizel* struck the reef. Out of seventy-eight passengers, only seventeen survived, and out of the crew of sixty there were but twenty-seven left.

CHAPTER **23**

*THE DAILY NEWS* had hit the streets early with screaming headlines and pictures of the *Florizel*, Captain Martin, and John Munn. It reported in great detail what was known of the disaster, and expressed puzzlement that she could have gotten so far off course as to wind up in such an unlikely part of the coast:

"To have reached Cappahayden at the hour the S.O.S. was sent out she must have made but very slow progress, and to get so far off her course may be due to accident to machinery, steering gear, or probably the loss of her propeller. It may be that she went ashore much earlier than the S.O.S. would suggest, and that it was impossible to send out the signal earlier. These are matters yet to be made known, but that some accident occurred is the general belief, as Captain Martin was looked on as one of the most careful navigators sailing from this port."

In the intervening hours between rescue and arrival in port, the names of the survivors were wirelessed to St. John's and posted outside the cable offices. Relatives of the lost still clung to the hope that somehow a mistake had been made.

It was a wretched group that landed in the port of St. John's. Hobbling on frostbitten feet, in makeshift dress, they were assisted ashore. The whole town had turned out to see who were the fortunate survivors, while frantic relatives darted forward to ask, fearfully, if so-and-so was alive. Women and children gave vent to their grief as the survivors, haggard and bedraggled, limped painfully to the Seamen's Institute on the waterfront, where a temporary hospital had been set up.

Most watched in silence, as they had four short years back, when the bodies of seal hunters, frozen in grotesque positions, had been brought ashore.* Captain Martin, assisted by the Honourable John Harvey and a brother, limped from the ship. A woman, unknown, stepped from the crowd. "Captain," she cried, *"what happened?"*

It was the last straw. Ninety-four people had lost their lives on the *Florizel*; many others had risked their lives to rescue them, and the responsibility lay at his door. In some unaccountable way he had driven a fine ship on the rocks and people had died, and now this unknown woman had faced him squarely with the question that was on thousands of lips.

Tears streamed down his cheeks. "Madam, I don't know," he cried. Overcome with grief, he allowed himself to be taken to the Seamen's Institute.

Phil Jackman was dispatched to the hospital. He was a ghastly sight, with no teeth, his nose hanging by the flesh and his face gashed. Those suffering frostbite and other injuries were also removed to the hospital; Joseph Burry's feet were frozen and Ralph Burnham's ten toes were broken from the jump into the dory and he would be a cripple for the rest of his life.

* See *Death on the Ice* by Cassie Brown with Harold Horwood.

Bolstered by family friends, the young Crockers had gone to the waterfront and mingled with the silent crowd as the survivors landed. Joe Burry's name had been on the list of survivors posted by the cable office, but their father's name had not. Amy firmly refused to accept the fact that the list was gospel; somehow, she told herself, her father's name had been overlooked.

Then they saw Joe being lifted over the side of the ship, and her brother John pushed his way through the crowd to reach him before he was taken away. Watching their faces, Amy knew that her father was lost.

Would her mother recover from this mortal blow?

Mary Jackman had not gone to the wharf where the ships had berthed; she had to stay at home to wait for Phil. He would walk in the front door as soon as it was humanly possible for him to make it; that she knew, so she waited in frozen silence, and at last her front door opened and a friend stood before her. "He's safe, Mary, but he's gone to the hospital."

She went immediately to the hospital. "He can't see you, Mrs. Jackman, and he may not recognize you at present, so you should stay only for a few minutes," the doctor told her.

Mary looked at the grotesque mask of bandages covering Phil's face and slipped her hand inside his big one resting on the counterpane. "Phil?" she whispered.

He squeezed her hand.

Mary Maloney had hidden her fears beneath a mask of calm dignity in front of her children. A hundred times on Sunday she had looked out over the bay and seen no change in the steep waves piling on the land. She had known too well what the seas were doing to the *Florizel* little more than twenty miles farther along the shore, and each time she looked she had died a little.

Young Albert had not left her throughout Sunday night. When her body demanded rest, he had watched over her. The dream had not recurred, but it was imprinted upon her mind, and kept her turning restlessly. The baby inside, reflecting her state of mind, kicked heavily.

When Gregory's name came over the telegraph wires as a survivor; the tears came in a flood. She felt giddy and light-headed, as though the top of her head had come off, and the dreadful pressure of the last twenty-four hours dissolved with her tears. Her warm, secure world settled back on its axis.

She laughed as she cried, and Albert, throwing his young arms awkwardly around her burgeoning body, laughed and cried with her.

PART V

# The
# Enquiry

# CHAPTER 24

RUMORS WERE rampant. The *Florizel* had been submarined by the Germans. The *Florizel* had not been *submarined* by the Germans, but they had sabotaged her by tampering with her compass. The reason it had taken her over nine hours to get from St. John's to Cappahayden was that she had been economizing on coal. Everyone had been roaring drunk before the ship left port. Captain Martin had been roaring drunk during the trip. He had not been *roaring* drunk, another rumor said, but he had been drinking with the passengers before leaving port, and so had the officers. The ship had been too close to shore. Captain Joe Kean had known she was too close to shore because of the wild motions of the ship. All the other captains aboard as passengers had known she was too close to shore and had roundly told Captain Martin so. All crew members had known she was too close to shore. Captain Martin had not wanted to leave port on Saturday until the storm had passed, another rumor said, but had been pressured to leave by Mr. Munn, who was anxious to join his wife in New York. And there was the surprise and shock that a twelve-knot ship had been steaming altogether for *over nine hours*, and had run ashore a mere three-to-four-hour run along the coast. Why? A man could *walk* the same distance in that time.

Her time was up, said others, because rats had been seen leaving the ship just before sailing time. There were murmurings, too, that the passengers — particularly the women and children — had been pretty much left to their own resources after the ship was wrecked. And, on the rising tide of rumor and insinuation, still another story reared its head: *the Florizel's engines had been tampered with*.

So the stories spread. There was acclaim for the splendid heroism of the men who effected the rescue, and all newspapers in their editorials urged the government to render them some form of recognition — the British Empire Medal perhaps.

The disaster hit world headlines. On March 1, the Meteorological Service of Ottawa bluntly charged those in authority over the *Florizel* with a disregard for official weather warnings. "The S. S. *Florizel* put to sea on Saturday last, ignoring the storm signals, and consequently the disaster and the accompanying terrible loss of life must be attributed to the sailing of the ship in the face of the warning of the Meteorological Services," it stated.

Disturbed by the rumors already flying about, the editor of the *Evening Telegram* took exception to the news release, which implied, he said in his editorial, that the *Florizel* was literally forced out of port in the teeth of a storm. "The real gravity lies in its direct assertion that the storm warnings were *deliberately* ignored, thereby leaving it to be assumed that those in charge of the ship and its precious cargo of human freight, were heedless of weather conditions."

This was a grave accusation and he strongly condemned it. "We must call for an investigation not only into the loss of the *Florizel*, but into the criminal negligence which for fifty years and more has left this hideous coastline without proper and sufficient aids to navigation," he wrote.

Because of the allegations by the Meteorological Services, a Commission of Enquiry was appointed with powers to investigate the conduct of not only the captain and crew of the *Florizel* but the owners and all other persons as well.

The Marine Court of Enquiry began March 5, 1918. It was under the jurisdiction of James P. Blackwood, K.C., with assistance from Commander Anthony MacDermott, R.N., Captain Edward English, and Captain George I. Spracklin. The Minister of Justice, the Honourable Dr. William Frederick Lloyd* and Mr. Brian Dunfield† represented the Crown; Mr. H. A. Winter§ and W. R. Warren# represented the owners of the *Florizel*; Mr. Michael Gibbs, K.C., a member of the Newfoundland Legislative Council, represented Captain William Martin and the ship's officers.

It was a gray, blustery day when Captain Martin stood before his peers. Pale and hollow-eyed, he faced some of the most brilliant lawyers in the land. The courtroom was jammed with spectators, curious to know the circumstances that had caused ninety-four people to die. For six grueling days he answered questions and, in minute detail, the Court examined the last voyage of the *Florizel*, from the moment of departure to the moment of disaster. Her capabilities, which were considerable, her faults (she appeared to have very few indeed), were laid bare as the Court went on to question every surviving member of the crew, and twelve of the surviv-

* Later Sir William F. Lloyd, Prime Minister of Newfoundland.
† Later Sir Brian Dunfield, Chief Justice of Newfoundland.
§ Later Speaker of House of Assembly.
# Later Attorney General of Newfoundland.

ing passengers in the following weeks. It soon became evident that the Germans had nothing whatever to do with the loss of the *Florizel*, and sabotage was ruled out, insofar as the compasses were concerned, when Martin stated that they had been in agreement when he sailed out The Narrows right up to Cape Spear, and at 4:00 A.M. when he had changed course to west by south, and, in his estimation, had not been tampered with. It was also evident that the *storm* was not the cause of the loss of the ship, but her *lack of speed*, with the greatest loss pinpointed from midnight to 4:00 A.M., when her speed had gone to an estimated low of six to seven knots, for which Martin could give no reasonable explanation.

"The wind would not hinder her, there wasn't that much wind anyhow, and I would like you to understand," he said earnestly, "that it would take an awful gale of wind with a head sea to bring the *Florizel* down to half speed."

There had been no gale of wind with a head sea. "I have often left port in worse weather and made better speed," he said emphatically.

"Perhaps," Lawyer Dunfield suggested, "there was a current working against the *Florizel*. Have you ever found the Polar Current to be reversed or interfered with?"

"No," Martin said, then changed his mind. "Once, many years ago when I was a young man before the mast, but not since."

"Would the sish ice have affected the ship?"

Martin was sure it had not. "It was only thick enough to keep the sea quiet," he said.

Commander MacDermott suggested that Martin could have overestimated the speed of the *Florizel* that night. "You had to judge the speed by looking at the water; could you be absolutely sure you were steaming at eight knots? Could you tell the difference of one knot, say between seven and eight knots?"

Martin confessed that he could not be sure if he could tell the difference of one knot. "But I could distinguish the difference of two knots for sure," he said.

"So it *is* possible that you overestimated the speed of the *Florizel*?" MacDermott asked.

Martin had to admit that it was possible.

Putting it together, Martin's possible overestimation of speed, and the probability of the Polar Current running against the *Florizel*, would definitely bring her speed down, but it could not account for her slow speed generally.

Questions took them in circles. Finally, Martin said that there was no logical reason for the *Florizel* to be steaming so slowly unless they did not have her out in full below.

"Please explain," Dunfield requested.

Martin looked acutely uncomfortable. "I had the telegraph on the bridge turned to 'Full Speed' but I don't know whether the engine was shut in* or not."

One could have heard a pin drop in the courtroom. To shut in the engine was not unusual in itself; what was unusual was that Captain Martin was intimating that it could have been done without his being informed of it.

"But surely," Dunfield said in astonishment, "there are orders to the engineers to inform you if they are unable to make the speed you ordered?"

"No," Martin replied, "there were no formal orders to the engine room."

For a man who had the reputation of being extremely careful and competent, Captain Martin did not appear to know what was going on aboard his ship. His image

* Throttled.

did not improve when he admitted that he knew nothing of the type or the characteristics of the ship's engine, or that he did not know how to estimate the speed of the ship by the revolutions of the screw as most captains could do in an emergency. "The engineers can explain all about that to you better than I," he told the Court.

How competent was the captain? Did it give credence to the stories of his drinking?

Lawyer Michael Gibbs asked, "Do you take a drink at sea, Captain Martin?"

"Not at sea," he replied. "I have made it a rule never to touch drink at sea."

"Then," Gibbs continued, "did you take a drink *the day you sailed?*"

"No, that is another rule I made, never to take a drink on sailing day."

"Did you take a drink *any time* during the voyage down the shore?" Gibbs asked.

"No," Martin replied firmly.

Later testimony given by the officers and crew satisfied the Court that Captain Martin had been alert and on the bridge off and on all night, and there were no further questions about his drinking habits.

While Martin sat in the pitiless glare of publicity, the sea grudgingly yielded its victims, and in small numbers they arrived daily from Cappahayden on what the newspapers called the "death train." Each day the bells tolled over St. John's, and large funeral processions paced to the various churches.

The sealing fleet was scheduled to sail at dawning on Monday, March 11, for the annual seal hunt at the icefields on the northeast coast of Newfoundland. On Saturday, March 9, the bodies of Joe Kean, John Munn, Betty Munn, Evelyn Trenchard, Tom McNeil, and Patrick Laracy were taken from the sea, and departure of the sealing fleet was postponed for half a day so that sealers could attend the funeral of Joe Kean on Monday morning — an unprecedented event in sealing history. The *Sable I* was in port with a new captain, but the sealers aboard were Joe's own tried and true men.

John Munn, Betty Munn, and Evelyn Trenchard were buried that afternoon. The funeral procession stirred afresh the rumors that John Munn had made Captain Martin leave port against his will.

The Court did not postpone the issue. "It has been stated that pressure was put upon you to sail when you did not wish to do so," Dunfield said. "Is that so?"

"That is wrong," Martin said.

"Leaving port was left to your own discretion?"

"Yes."

Bluntly: "Did the presence of Mr. Munn on board the *Florizel* influence you in any way?"

"He had nothing whatever to do with it," Martin stated flatly. Leaving port was his own decision, he said.

There was one point that would later conflict with other testimony. Dunfield asked him if he had taken soundings after leaving Cape Spear.

He replied, "Yes, I took soundings after Mr. Jackman told me she was sagging into Petty Harbor Bay and he had hauled her out perhaps a quarter or half point. I had to find out where we were, so I ordered the sounding tube out."

Like a hound sniffing prey, MacDermott leaned forward, his voice steely: "Have the officers of the watch *any right* to alter the ship's course except in cases of emergency, without your permission?"

Such an action was obviously a serious offense, and MacDermott belabored the point in spite of Martin's insistence that he had given Jackman the authority to do so. The whole procedure, which had been an ordinary one on the *Florizel*, seemed to have taken on serious proportions that could bode ill for his younger officer. He was relieved when MacDermott changed the subject: "Did the *Florizel* make much leeway?"*

"No," Martin replied, "she's a wonderful ship to make to windward."

"Even with her cutaway bow?" MacDermott was skeptical. All ships fall off their course; the *Florizel's* specially designed bow would make her even more susceptible, in his estimation.

But Martin said stubbornly, "Even with her cutaway bow."

In order for the *Florizel* to strike Horn Head Reef, it was deduced that in spite of the change of course at midnight from southwest-quarter-south to south-southwest (one and three-quarter points), the *Florizel* had made absolutely no headway on the south-southwest course. Because of her extremely slow speed, she had not steamed forward on her course away from land, but had been pushed along the coast a mere *quarter point* southward of the course she had had been steaming up to midnight.

William Dooley made notorious headlines on March 21 when he was arrested for the alleged murder of Robert Penney, a returned soldier, in a street fight. Dooley had knocked the man down; they had been quickly separated and Penney had gone his way, but had hemorrhaged later that night and died.

The townspeople were shocked. Dooley, the hero who had offered to risk his life by swimming ashore with Captain Martin, *a murderer*? His arrest brought

* A falling off from the line of progress.

mixed reactions in the press, and he was let out on ten thousand dollars bail two days later.

Third Officer Philip Jackman was very self-conscious about his mutilated, swollen face, which seemed to be stitched and taped together, and it was obviously still painful for him to talk. He corroborated Captain Martin's story in every way but one: "I did not change the ship's course at any time," he stated.

"But this sagging in . . . ?" MacDermott began.

"I *thought* she was sagging in, but she was not," he said.

Either Jackman or Martin had lied, but the Court did not pursue it.

Jackman could give no plausible explanation for the ship's slow speed. "Did you not think it was *strange* that she was not doing more than she was?" MacDermott asked.

Jackman shifted uneasily, "It looks as if there was something strange about it now, all right," he answered.

First Officer William James, questioned at length, was not prepared to say that the sish ice cut down on the *Florizel's* speed by any definite number of knots; nor was he prepared to submit to any speculation as to why her progress had been so slow. "I cannot give any theory at all," he said flatly.

The question was: Why, after more than nine hours' steaming, was the *Florizel* less than fifty miles from port?

The engineers verified that the *Florizel's* engine had been in excellent condition, but seemed unable to explain that great drop in speed. Fourth Engineer Herbert Taylor did make one odd statement when asked by the

Court how the engine was working when leaving port. He stated: "Everything was in okay condition when Lumsden was in charge."

He was not asked to explain that remark, which seemed to imply that all was *not* well after Second Engineer Thomas Lumsden went off duty around nine o'clock, or, that as the junior engineer, he was less efficient than Lumsden.

Third Engineer Eric Collier testified that while the racing of the screw, in his watch, had not been exceptional, it would have brought her revolutions down and slowed the speed of the ship. This explained the drop from sixty-nine to sixty-three revolutions in the middle watch, but did nothing to clarify the reason for her slow speed generally.

Thomas Lumsden took the stand on a stormy Saturday. Outside, the wind howled around the great stone building, snow was clogging the streets, but the courtroom was as crowded as usual, for if rumor had any foundation, the root cause of the disaster lay in the engine room and everybody expected Lumsden to clear up the mystery.

He did not. When asked what would cause the speed of the engine to drop to sixty-three revolutions in the middle watch, he vaguely supposed it was the heavy weather, and went on to say that heavy weather, wind, ship's rolling, would make a difference to the ship's engine; they did not plow as easily through the sea, and there was always slip in the propeller. He explained "slip" as the difference between the speed of the engine and the speed of the propeller when the screw was not driving solidly through the water. There was some slip in all propellers, he said, and driving against heavy seas, speed was lost in revolutions *and* slip.

MacDermott asked, "Would you say that the general

loss of speed was owing to the weather the ship was meeting?"

Lumsden conceded only that it *might* have been.

Dissatisfied with Martin's claims that there were no routine formal orders between bridge and engine room, MacDermott questioned Lumsden about it. Lumsden was quite explicit: If there was trouble in the engine room it was reported to the chief only.

MacDermott was astounded. "You would not report it to the bridge?"

"No, I would leave that to the chief."

"Doesn't the engineer of the watch make *any report whatever* to the bridge?"

"No."

"*Never?*" MacDermott could hardly believe his ears.

"No."

"Is it not the usual thing for the engineer of the watch to give the number of engine revolutions to the bridge?"

It was not. Every noon the chief engineer and the captain would get together and exchange notes, but not every watch, Lumsden said.

More than ever it was looking as if Captain Martin did not have complete command of his ship. The Court brought forward Dave MacFarlane, a Scot with a first-class English Board of Trade Certificate. He was also surveyor of machinery for Lloyds of London and the British Corporation. MacFarlane was familiar with the *Florizel's* engine.

Blackwood asked, "Can you tell us why the revolutions, in a steamer like the *Florizel* whose full number of revolutions at full speed was seventy-five a minute, should be sixty-three in one watch, sixty-nine in another watch, or generally why the number of revolutions should vary at all?"

MacFarlane countered with a question of his own.

"Do you know whether she was fully opened out? Do you know whether the chief engineer had adjusted her valve gear and so reduced the number of possible revolutions whilst carrying the same pressure?"

"Would an engineer reduce the number of possible revolutions *without reporting to the captain?*" Blackwood asked.

"Well, I have done it," MacFarlane replied. Chief engineers sometimes reduced the revolutions without informing the captain, he said. "He might *intend* to report it, of course, and let the matter slip his mind."

Blackwood asked smoothly, "But what object could the chief engineer of the *Florizel* have had on her last voyage in reducing the revolutions?"

MacFarlane gave it his consideration. "There might be some part of machinery he might want to ease up on, or, since the *Florizel* just had a new propeller, he might want to try what his new propeller would do *at those revolutions.*"

In other words, the weather conditons had not reduced her revolutions that drastically, but they had been deliberately reduced for some reason.

Lumsden was recalled and bluntly asked: "Was the gear valve on board the *Florizel* adjusted?"

"No, sir," Lumsden replied.

Other than pointing the finger of guilt in the general direction of the engine room, the Enquiry seemed to be getting nowhere. It did not make sense that her revolutions had been cut down, but there was no other reason for her slow speed.

John Edward Tucker, Chief Officer of the *Florizel*, quarantined prior to the last voyage, was called to the stand. He was as familiar with the *Florizel* as anyone.

Dunfield asked, "As far as you know the conditions with regard to the wind, sea, and ice, were they sufficient to account, to your mind, for the *Florizel* taking nearly nine hours to get from St. John's to Cappahayden?"

Tucker said flatly, "No."

Blackwood asked, "If you had been on the ship during the first watch and her speed was only eight knots after her ashes were blown out, what would you have done?"

"I would have asked the chief engineer what he was doing with it," was Tucker's blunt reply.

Evidence pointed directly to Chief Engineer Reader, but no further light was shed on the issue. One thing stood out clearly: Captain Martin had not asserted his authority that night. Something had been amiss on his ship, but he had taken no positive measures to combat it.

The Court recalled him to ask why he had not made inquiries of the engine room about the *Florizel's* slow speed.

He replied, "I have never had occasion to go to the engine room. The Chief was one of the most competent men I ever met and if there was anything wrong he would come and tell me." He reiterated, "I had the utmost confidence in him."

The Court had nowhere to go from there.

With the assistance of Captain Luke Holmes,* who worked on a chart with Captain Martin giving the course he thought the ship had sailed, and with Holmes working backward from where the ship had struck, the Court concluded that if Martin had sounded when he changed course to west-southwest at 4:00 A.M. at the point where he thought he was, he would have gotten eighty-one fathoms. If he had sounded twenty minutes

---

* Of Saint John, New Brunswick.

later he would have gotten eighty-four fathoms and would have carried on to deeper water for six or seven miles. If Captain Martin had sounded at the point where he actually was steaming at four o'clock, his first sounding would have given him eighty-one fathoms, his second sounding would have given him forty-five fathoms, his third sounding would have warned him very much that he was approaching land.

Rescue operations came under the scrutiny of the Court. Why had the rescue ships taken so long to get operational? It was conceded that, had the ships been at Cappahayden in the afternoon of Sunday, February 24, survivors could have been removed from the wreck then, instead of having to wait until the following morning. No decisive action had been taken in the early stages of the rescue operation; everybody appeared to be waiting for the official seal of approval before proceeding.

Commander MacDermott was not asked to look into the cause of the delayed arrival of the reservists aboard the rescue ships, which could have left port much earlier had they been immediately available. The facts were recorded; no conclusions were drawn.

In spite of the laggardly start of the rescue, the Newfoundland Naval Reservists had done outstanding work, above and beyond the call of duty, and along with other seamen of the rescue ships received the Royal Humane Society Medal for Bravery at Sea in August, 1919, when the Prince of Wales* visited Newfoundland.

Nobody would point the finger at the man who refused to let Kitty Cantwell in the Marconi house. Minnie De-

* Later the Duke of Windsor.

nief told the Court that she heard someone say: "That is a woman, open the door!"

Albert Fagan testified that when Kitty pounded on the door someone had said the place was filled up, but both he and Minnie were behind the crowd, and did not know who was holding the door. Whether it was a passenger or a crew member was never made known.

The Court inquired of each witness whether he had difficulty getting into the Marconi room; all said no except Joseph Moore, who received an outright refusal after he got up through the skylight. The Court decided that Miss Cantwell's statement that she had at first been refused admission had been incorrect. "There may have been a delay of a minute or two in getting the door open, but there cannot be any doubt that she was admitted as promptly as practicable," was the verdict.

Which did not alter the fact that someone *had* refused her admittance in the first place.

Many questions were to be answered: Were safe and proper courses set? Was due and proper allowance made for leeway? For wind, sea, and ice? For the effect of tide and current? Were the distances run by the ship correctly estimated? Was the master competent? Was the Polar Current reversed? Was a light seen at 3:00 A.M.? Had all due endeavors been made by the master, officers, and crew for the safety of the passengers? Was the *Florizel's* engine revolving at its usual speed, and if not, to what extent were they slowed, and why?

# CHAPTER 25

*THE CROWN* studied the evidence and retraced the *Florizel's* last voyage down the coast. Working with charts, meticulously establishing distances from one point to another, Lawyer Dunfield deduced that Captain Martin had overestimated the speed of his ship by a knot or a knot and a half.

The slob ice, which the captain and his officers said was not heavy enough to impede the *Florizel* had, in Mr. Dunfield's estimation, thickened as it was driven inshore by the wind, and had carried the *Florizel* shoreward.

Captain Martin did not allow enough for leeway, Dunfield charged. The *Florizel* did have a tendency to leeway, for in setting his course, the captain had allowed a quarter point to windward in order to maintain a correct southwest course. "The allowance was of doubtful sufficiency," he said, "because the officer of the watch thought she was sagging into Petty Harbor Bay. *The ship continued to sag steadily inshore from 9:45 P.M. to midnight*, and further," he charged, "that on account of the steadily increasing density of the slob ice as it was driven upon the land, the speed of the ship *progressively decreased.*"

Therefore, at midnight, when the captain supposed himself to be at a point between three and four miles northward of Cape Broyle, he was, in reality, six to eight miles *northward* of that point, and between one and two miles inside of his course. "Her speed continued to decrease, dropping to a low of four knots between midnight and 1:00 A.M. when the wind was blowing up to thirty-six miles an hour, and getting up to four and a half knots as the wind dropped slightly at two o'clock," he said.

In spite of the offshore course at midnight, which should have taken her out into the Atlantic away from land, she was carried steadily landward to a point where Ferryland light would be from three to four miles upon her starboard quarter. He felt this was the light seen by Hatchard and King. "The fact of their having supposed that they saw this light independently, and in the same direction, goes very strongly to support that it was, in fact, a real light."

The heavy rolling of the ship from four o'clock onward was attributed to the fact that she had actually been on, or very close to, the Bullhead Bantems and the Renews Bantems.

That the captain should err so greatly in the ship's speed was due in large measure to the fact that he had not taken into consideration the possibility of the reversed Polar Current, which would have flowed against the *Florizel* at the rate of one knot, *and* his overestimation of speed, Dunfield said. The ship never reached the speed of eight knots once she turned Cape Spear, but had steamed at six and a quarter knots only. Chart measurements verified this.

Dunfield conceded that Captain Martin would not be able to detect the reversal of the Polar Current without sight of some fixed point of land, and that soundings from Cape Spear to an area south of Ferryland, being very even, were of little help to him in determining his position in the darkness of night. "However," Dunfield said, "a series of soundings from his actual position at midnight to 5:00 A.M. would have shown the captain he was not upon the course he thought he was on."

Although reversal of the Polar Current was a rare event, a master who was responsible for a passenger ship *should have allowed for all possible influences known to him*, Dunfield charged. "In view of the heavy and thick weather and the possible current, and the fact that he was unable to use his log and was not accustomed to use the revolutions of his propeller to estimate distance, *and* that he had not seen land for six hours, *he was not entitled to regard as safely fixed, a point for changing course towards land*."

Dunfield felt that having changed course toward land, Captain Martin should have reduced speed and sounded continually. "For this lack of caution, I submit he may be held to blame," he said.

PART VI

# Judgment

# CHAPTER 26

*THEY THREW* the book at Captain William Martin.

Said James Blackwood, "I am of the opinion that the master was in default in not verifying his position by sounding before changing his course from south-southwest at 4:00 A.M.; or if he could not have done so before changing course, *in not reducing his speed and verifying his position* by constantly sounding after changing.

"In this case, if no other means of fixing his position were available, he could have waited until daylight if necessary, to ascertain his position. In very thick weather daylight might have helped him but little. On *this* occasion, however, *it would have disclosed to him his whereabouts*, and every case must be judged by its own circumstances and the measures for safety presently available.

"The casualty is attributable to the master's default in not taking these precautions, and considering the magnitude of the disaster, the loss of life and property, his Master's Certificate is suspended for twenty-one months, but in view of his good record and general care and attention to duty, the Court thinks he should be allowed a Chief Mate's Interim Certificate for the time of suspension."

The Court also considered the *Florizel's* course unnecessarily close to shore; due allowance had not been made for leeway, or for the effect of sea and swell in the middle watch. Captain Martin had not been able to make use of the number and speed of the revolutions in estimating the speed or distance run by the ship, and displayed incompetence in this area.

Blackwood was dissatisfied that there was no explanation why the engine recorded only sixty-three revolutions in the middle watch, or why seventy-five revolutions were not made with a full head of steam. "I am forced to assume that it is not altogether unusual," he said.

Evidence with regard to the supposed flash of light seen at 3:00 A.M. by King and Hatchard was considered too flimsy to be taken into account.

Blackwood decided that, in spite of rumors to the contrary, all due endeavors were made by the master, officers, and crew for the safety of the passengers.

The Court decided that the natural forces which operated on the *Florizel* to slow her down on that final voyage were (1) the wind and weather, (2) the sea, (3) the reversal of the usual southwesterly Polar Current. The question of the sish ice having any effect on her speed was eliminated, as the evidence of crew and passengers seemed to negate it.

However, the Enquiry ended on a note of dissatisfaction: *"Exactly what happened on the* Florizel *throughout the night of February 23, 24, will never be known."*

The mystery was still there, though the answer to it seemed to lie in the *Florizel's* engine room. Captain Martin had said: "I don't know if she was shut in." His orders had been for full speed but he was intimating that it was possible his orders had been disregarded. First Officer John Tucker stated bluntly that *he* would have asked the chief engineer what he was doing with the engines, but the Court did not recall any of the engineers to directly ask if she had been shut in. They had asked Lumsden if the valve gears had been adjusted, but did not ask if she had been throttled or slowed in.

Officially it was over, but the rumors persisted. The Enquiry had come to its own conclusions, but the surviving seamen knew what they knew. An Enquiry could ask a million questions and still steer around the heart of the matter, and, they said to their relatives and friends, Mr. Munn *had* ordered Captain Martin to sea; Captain Martin *had* been drinking with the passengers at the farewell party before leaving port, but was by no means drunk; the crew *had* been uneasy during the middle watch because they knew by the ship's wild movements she was in shallow water. The storm had not been of the intensity to cause such severe motion unless they *were* in shallow water. All of these things they knew and spoke of freely amongst themselves, and they *knew* that the engine had been tampered with.

On the other side of the coin, if John Munn *had* ordered the *Florizel* out, she was a strong, sturdy ship, more than capable of holding her own in any weather; if Captain Martin drank at sea, it was a fact that the majority of sea captains took their tots regularly; it was an old British naval tradition. Who could deny sailors needed fortification of some kind to withstand the frigid blasts of the North Atlantic?

So matters stood.

Dooley went on trial for murder in May, 1918, and was found not guilty.

The Court submitted recommendations that another

257

Court of Enquiry be appointed to visit the southeast coast and report as to suitable localities for the institution of more lights, fog signals, and life-saving stations.

Nothing was done. The Prime Minister, Sir Edward Patrick Morris,* had resigned and the Newfoundland Government was in a constant state of upheaval. In January, 1919, it was brought before the Government again, but there the matter died.

In 1953 the Canadian Government placed a light on Northern Head near Fermeuse, and finally, in 1964, another light was placed in Renews Harbour. The Newfoundland people are still waiting for life-saving stations.

Six bodies were never recovered, among them the deaf mute Clarence Moulton. The body of Billy Guzzwell was found one year later on the beach of Cappahayden. The remains were identified only by the stockings knitted by his grandmother.

Kitty Cantwell never set foot aboard a ship again. She married Mike McDonald in the fall of 1918. She died in 1974.

In February, 1919, almost a year to the day later, Minnie Denief sailed to New York on the S. S. *Prospero*; she was married the following year. She died in the late 1960's. Throughout her lifetime she suffered continually with her feet.

John Johnston went to sea for several years, but later operated a restaurant, then a garage. He died in the mid-1950's.

The name of Betty Munn still lives, perpetuated in memory by a replica of Sir George Frampton's statue of Peter Pan, erected in her honor, in the fifty-acre park that had been presented to the city of St. John's by Sir Edgar Bowring in 1911.

* Later Baron Morris.

Captain William Martin left Newfoundland and never returned; he settled in Brooklyn, New York, and, because of his previous excellent record, was quickly accepted by the Munson Lines and, later, Wessel Duvol. His trips as master were to ports in South America. In later years, when visited by old shipmates,* he told them he *knew* why the *Florizel* had gone ashore, but would say no more.

He never spoke of the tragedy to his two sons, William and Robert. They learned of it through friends, sailors, and Newfoundlanders who settled in Brooklyn in the years that followed. When Captain Martin was not at sea, his sons remembered him as spending a few hours each evening praying in the parish church close by. He was Port Captain when he died of a stroke, January 20, 1939, at the age of sixty-three.

Fourth Engineer Herbert Taylor suffered from indifferent health after the wreck. He received his second engineer's certificate, but died of tuberculosis in 1928 at the age of thirty-two. Engineers Lumsden and Collier lived their normal lifespan, and so did Philip Jackman, but Jackman was scarred, outwardly and inwardly, for he carried in his breast a terrible secret.

Adored by his wife, loved by his friends, and looked upon with great respect and admiration by the junior officers of the ships he sailed, Jackman eventually could not bear the burden of the secret, and to a select few he revealed the truth. The story filtered down through the years, remaining in the tight confines of marine circles.

Captain Thomas Goodyear — a junior officer in the late 1930's — had served on the *Rosalind* and spent a few years under the benevolent eye of "Uncle Phil" Jackman. The physical scars had all but disappeared from

* As revealed by Thomas Metcalfe.

Jackman's face, but the psychic scars remained, and it was evident on the anniversary of the *Florizel* disaster each year: he became a different man and did not encourage the younger officers to come around. He made it clear that he wanted to be alone, and it was conceded that he spent a very uncomfortable night of it.

The young officers were curious at the remarkable change that came over the benign first officer. There was no doubt that he was restless, uneasy, and uncommunicative, and they respected his feelings, leaving him completely alone.

But why? they queried their senior officers.

Because, the senior officers said, "Uncle Phil" always blamed himself for the loss of the *Florizel*.

And for these young sailors, the mystery unfolded.

*February 23/24, 1918*
At midnight Philip Jackman left the bridge and went to the officers' duty mess for a snack before turning in. He was having tea and toast when the third engineer came into the mess for a cup of tea. They chatted for a few minutes and during their conversation it was disclosed that Reader had reduced the engine revolutions a little.

If they had continued on at their normal full speed the *Florizel* would have arrived in port Monday afternoon. With the small amount of cargo to be discharged there, she would have been on her way to New York the same evening. Reader's family lived in Halifax and their home had been badly shattered by the huge explosion that had demolished the city in December, although the family had survived. Wishing to spend Monday night with them, the chief had slowed the ship in to delay her arrival in port by a few hours.

Jackman's first impulse was to return to the bridge and pass the information to the captain — it was his duty to do so — but caution prevailed. As the junior officer aboard, dare he presume to approach the captain with suggestions that the engine had been slowed in? There were other considerations too: It would put the chief on the spot, probably get the third engineer in trouble, and create bad feeling between the bridge and the engine room.

While these were not exactly minor considerations in the interrelations aboard ship, Jackman's main concern was Captain Martin. If the captain had not already given thought to the possibility of her being slowed in, it could imply that he was less than competent. Martin was a "foreign-going" master, an entirely different breed of sailor from the Newfoundland coastal captains, less approachable and less likely to appreciate a word from his junior officer. He might well *fire* Jackman when they returned to port.

On top of that, Jackman brooded, it would be betraying a confidence, however casually given.

It was one hell of a spot to be in.

But there was no thought of disaster and no cause for alarm. It was not stormy by seamen's standards, and the *Florizel* was steaming away from land on a south-southwest course. The captain was making allowance for the slow speed anyway.

Jackman decided to leave it alone.

For this reason, Philip Jackman always felt that he was, to a great degree, responsible for the loss of the *Florizel*.

Jackman's situation was a peculiar one. In his private estimation the *Florizel's* course that night, when she turned Cape Spear, had been too close to shore and, when she sagged in on the land, he *had* hauled her out as Captain Martin testified but, intimidated by MacDermott's insinuation that he had overstepped the bounds of his authority, he denied it. Later he told his wife that if he had *not* hauled her out, her course would probably have taken her right to the Renews Rocks, and *all* would have been lost.

In the light of Jackman's revelation, the odd statements made during the Enquiry can be explained. Captain Martin's conjecture that maybe she was "shut in" (or throttled), suggests that he suspected she had been. Knowing the chief and his family well, perhaps he suspected that the engines had been slowed in for personal reasons and allowed more than three extra hours to compensate for it. Undoubtedly, Jackman and the engineers revealed the facts to him when it was all over.

Fourth Engineer Taylor who said, "Everything was in okay condition when Lumsden was in charge," undoubtedly meant exactly that. It suggests that after the ashes were ejected, the chief came to the engine room and throttled her. From that time on, everything was *not* okay. Technically, the fourth engineer's watch was the chief's watch, and the chief's decision was law.

Mechanically, the engine was operating perfectly and, bearing in mind that even sixty-three revolutions would normally give the *Florizel* a speed of nine to ten knots, she had been slowed in only a little, but her speed had been further reduced by the reversal of the Polar Current and, because of it, she was less able to cope with the effect of wind, sea and ice.

All of this presupposes collusion among the crew at the Enquiry. Most likely, under the directive of Captain Martin, they did not volunteer information that would involve the chief. No matter what the circumstances, the blame for the disaster still lay with him as master.

And rightly so. No matter how much she had been slowed in, the simple use of the sounding lead would have averted the tragedy.

As Sir C. Alexander Harris, Governor of Newfoundland, wrote in a confidential dispatch to Downing Street, London, England: "The Enquiry was most carefully conducted by the Commissioner and his Assessors, but the result reduced itself into the comparatively simple issue of an unaccountable failure of judgment on the part of a man who had been reputed a most careful mariner."

A new regulation, stipulating that the engine room must report the engine's revolutions to the bridge at the end of each watch, was enforced after the loss of the *Florizel*. Since that time, anything out of the normal is immediately reported to the bridge.

Nevertheless . . .

Engines are still "slowed in" for personal reasons, and there is an unspoken agreement that no questions be asked *unless* the captain suspects that he has a chief engineer who is not as competent as he should be. Then there is contention between bridge and engine room.

If the chief is a capable man, no captain will trample the delicate boundary that separates the bridge from the engine room, and when it is the bridge that requests delay of arrival in port for personal reasons, the favor is returned.

It is never entered in the logbook.

The *Florizel* wintered many a storm. Held to the reef by the smokestack, her protesting clatters could be heard in the tiny community of Cappahayden when the wind was right. In spite of the fierce seas of that unfriendly shore, the Marconi house was still standing the following summer. For years she lay on the reef until sea and ice eventually battered her to pieces. Her remains lie in the water surrounding Horn Head.

To this day, old people in St. John's remember the

strange feeling that came over them when they heard the plaintive sound of her whistle as she sailed through The Narrows that fateful night. *They* say the *Florizel* knew that her time had come.

# APPENDIX 1

# Those Who Died

*Passengers*

James H. Baggs (40), Curling, Bay of Island.
Miss Mabel Barrett (23), St. John's.
Captain James Bartlett (25) Bay Roberts, Conception Bay.
Blanche Beaumont (11), St. John's.
Captain O. P. Belleveau (38), Weymouth, Nova Scotia.
Edward Berteau, St. John's.
William E. Bishop (48), Burin.
Wilbert Butler (35), St. John's.
William F. Butler (50), St. John's.
Mrs. William F. Butler (40), St. John's.
Frank Chown (19), St. John's.
John Connolly (31), St. John's.
Michael Connolly (74), St. John's.
John Costello (49), Conception Harbor, Conception Bay.
James Crockwell, Bay Bulls.
James Daley (40), St. John's.
Miss Annie Dalton (33), Western Bay
William Earle (42), Fogo, Notre Dame Bay.
Patrick J. Fitzpatrick (42), Argentia, Placentia Bay.
John Forrest (23), Charlottetown, P.E.I.
R.J. Fowlow (30), Cupids, Conception Bay.

Edgar Froude (38), St. John's.
Edward Greening (36), Bonavista.
Peter Guilfoyle (27), Harbour Grace.
Billy Guzzwell (11), St. John's.
Charles Howell (24), Trinity, Trinity Bay.
Captain Joseph Kean (44), St. John's.
Patrick Laracy (50), St. John's.
George Long (37), St. John's.
John Lynch (55), Bay Bulls.
John Maloney (7 months), St. John's.
Joseph Maloney (29), St. John's.
Mrs. Joseph (Mary) Maloney (28), St. John's.
George Massie (41), Chicago, Ill.
Mrs. George Massie (38), Chicago, Ill.
Katherine Massie (8), Chicago, Ill.
James J. McCoubrey (40), St. John's.
Thomas McMurdo McNeil (45), St. John's.
C. H. Miller (42), St. John's.
James Miller (30), St. John's.
William Moore, St. John's.
Clarence E. Moulton (7), St. John's.
George A. (Bert) Moulton (33), St. John's.
Betty Munn (3½), St. John's.
John Shannon Munn (37), St. John's.
Leonard Nicholls (31), St. John's.
Michael O'Driscoll (37), St. John's.
George Parmiter, Harbour Grace.
Jack C. Parsons (27), St. John's.
Miss Elizabeth Pelley (29), Smith Sound, Trinity Bay.
Heber Piercey (22), Western Bay.
Andy Power (24), Argentia, Placentia Bay.
George Puddester (42), Bay Bulls.
Walter J. Richards (24), La Have, Nova Scotia.
Gerald St. John (20), St. John's.
Newman Sellars (20), St. John's.
F. C. Smythe (40), St. John's.

Fred Snow (22), St. John's.
George E. Stevenson (53), New York.
Miss Evelyn Trenchard (30), St. John's.
Robert Wright (45), St. John's.


*Crew*

Charles Bailey, A.B., Port Rexton, Trinity Bay.
F. Beguere, fireman, Spain.
George Crocker, A.B., Greenspond.
Michael Dunphy, waiter, St. John's.
Stanley Foley, waiter, St. John's.
Francisco Fornas, fireman, Spain.
Tomas Garcia, fireman, Spain.
Arthur Gover, A.B., Trinity.
Alegrandro Grierio, fireman, Spain.
Fred Gutherie, 2nd cook, Liverpool, England.
Thomas Hennebury, oiler, St. John's.
Gordon Ivany, waiter, St. John's.
Margaret Keough, stewardess, St. John's.
John R. King, Second Officer, Arichat, Nova Scotia.
John Lambert, A.B., St. John's.
Patrick Lynch, waiter, St. John's.
Joseph McKinnon, baker, St. John's.
  (Formerly Glasgow, Scotland).
José Mendez, fireman, Spain.
A. Moody, baker, Hampshire, England.
John Power, A.B., Paradise, Conception Bay.
John V. Reader, Chief Engineer, Halifax, N.S.
Francisco Reguira, fireman, Spain.
Ramon Rez, fireman, Spain.
Enrique Rodriguez, fireman, Spain.
Gerardo Rodriguez, fireman, Spain.
Manuel Rodriguez, fireman, Spain.
Charles Snow, second steward, St. John's.

José Soane, fireman, Spain.
Stanley Squires, waiter, St. John's.
José Vila, fireman, Spain.
William Walters, A.B., Trinity.
Austin Whitten, waiter, St. John's.
Manuel Yannez, fireman, Spain.

*Bodies not recovered*

Francisco Fornas, fireman, Spain.
Edward Greening, Bonavista.
Charles Howell, Trinity.
Gordon Ivany, St. John's.
Clarence E. Moulton, St. John's.
Leonard Nicholls, St. John's.

# APPENDIX 2

# Those Who Survived

*Passengers*

Ralph Burnham (23) St. John's.
Miss Kitty Cantwell (21) St. John's.
John Cleary (27) Argentia, Placentia Bay.
Noah Dauphinee (36), Tantillion County, Nova Scotia.
Miss Minnie Denief (21), St. John's.
William Dodd (22), Torbay.
Albert G. Fagan (29), St. John's.
Archibald E. Gardiner (30), Britannia Cove, Trinity Bay.
Dave Griffiths (24), Long Harbour, Placentia Bay.
John P. Kieley (32), St. John's.
Alex Ledingham (30), St. John's.
Gregory Maloney (45), Bay Bulls.
William Parmiter (40), St. John's.
John G. Sparrow (27) Argentia, Placentia Bay.
Joseph Stockley (22), Bonavista.
Major Michael S. Sullivan (42), St. John's.
Thomas Whelan (27), Torbay.

*Crew*

Seaman Joseph Burry (33), Greenspond.
Wireless Operator Cecil Sidney Carter, New York.
Third Engineer Eric Collier (26), St. John's.
Gunner George Henry Curtis (36)
   Hythe, Southampton, England.
Oiler John Davis, St. John's.
Waiter Henry Dodd (21), St. John's.
Seaman William Dooley (34), St. John's.
Waiter James Dwyer (26), St. John's.
Fireman José Fernandez, New York
Waiter Alex Fleet (24), St. John's.
Seaman Thomas Green, Fermeuse.
Gunner Alfred Hatchard (33), Poole, England.
Third Officer Philip Jackman (31), St. John's.
First Officer William James (35), St. John's.
Pantry Waiter John Johnston, (22), St. John's.
Second Engineer Thomas Lumsden, (35), St. John's.
Captain William Martin, (43), St. John's.
Seaman William Molloy, (29), Cape Broyle.
Cook Joseph Moore, St. John's.
Wireless Operator Bernard John Murphy, (24),
   Liverpool, England.
Carpenter Jacob Pinsent, (32),
   Pool's Island, Greenspond.
Boatswain Michael F. Power, St. John's.
Waiter Charlie Reelis, (23), St. John's.
Cook Fred Roberts, (27), St. John's.
Waiter Henry Snow, (22), St. John's.
Fourth Engineer Herbert Taylor, (22), St. John's.
Oiler Edward Timmons, St. John's.

# Recipients of the Royal Humane Society Medal for Bravery at Sea

The S. S. *Gordon C*

Captain E. C. Perry
Chief Engineer Robert Pierson
Seaman Joseph Budden


The S. S. *Hawk*

Captain Martin Dalton
Seaman Daniel Ralph
Seaman Michael Whelan

The S. S. *Terra Nova*

Seaman Harold Clouter
Seaman Patrick Gallagher
Seaman Loil Hann
Seaman George Mercer
Seaman John R. Moores
Seaman Aldolphus Morey
Seaman Timothy Murphy
Seaman Charles W. Penney
Seaman Matthew Shanahan
Seaman George Westcott


The S. S. *Prospero*

Captain Eugene Burden
Captain William Windsor
Chief Officer Elisha Saunders
Chief Engineer James McKinley
Second Officer Joshua Warford
Boatswain William L. Crocker
Steward A. Starkes
Seaman Sidney Giles
Seaman Frank Walsh
Seaman M. Walsh
Fireman W. Ashman
Donkeyman W. O'Toole

The S. S. *Home*

Captain M. Day
Seaman Edgar Button
Seaman Samuel Cooper
Seaman Stephen Nash
Seaman Walter J. Nash
Seaman Walter S. Reid
Seaman Michael Woodford

# Witnesses at the Enquiry

*Crew*

Joseph Burry, Seaman.
Cecil Sidney Carter, Wireless Operator.
Eric Collier, Third Engineer.
George Henry Curtis, Gunner.
John Davis, Oiler.
Henry Dodd, Waiter.
William Dooley, Seaman.
James Dwyer, Waiter.
José Fernandez, Fireman.
Alex Fleet, Waiter.
Thomas Green, Quartermaster.
Alfred Hatchard, Gunner.
William James, Mate.
John Johnston, Waiter.
Thomas Lumsden, Second Engineer.
William Martin, Captain.
Joseph Moore, Cook.
William Molloy, Boatswain.
Bernard John Murphy, Wireless Operator.
Jacob Pinsent, Seaman.
Michael Power, Boatswain.

Charlie Reelis, Waiter.
Fred Snow, Cook.
Henry Snow, Steward.
Herbert Taylor, Fourth Engineer.
Edward Timmons, Oiler.
John Edward Tucker, Chief Officer.


*Passengers*

Miss Kitty Cantwell
Noah Dauphinee
Miss Minnie Denief
Albert Fagan
Archibald Gardiner
Dave Griffiths
J. P. Kieley
Alex Ledingham
William Parmiter
Joseph Stockley
Michael S. Sullivan


*Others*

Dr. Alex Campbell
William Carter
Frederick Cornick
John W. Costello
The Honourable John C. Crosbie,
    Minister of Shipping
Martin Dalton, Captain
George Findley, Captain
Fred Foote, Chief Engineer
The Honourable John Harvey,
    Director of Harvey and Company

Luke Holmes, Captain
Dave McFarlane
Thomas McGrath
Ernest Perry, Captain
Marcus Simonsen, Captain
The Honourable John G. Stone,
  Minister of Marine and Fisheries
Cyril Tessier

ECHEANCE     DATE DUE